# Disregard First Book

## Terry Martin Hekker

iUniverse, Inc.
New York   Bloomington

# DISREGARD FIRST BOOK

iUniverse books may be ordered through booksellers or by contacting:

iUniverse
1663 Liberty Drive
Bloomington, IN 47403
www.iuniverse.com
1-800-Authors (1-800-288-4677)

Because of the dynamic nature of the Internet, any Web addresses or links contained in this book may have changed since publication and may no longer be valid.

ISBN: 978-1-4401-3124-0 (pbk)
ISBN: 978-1-4401-3125-7 (ebk)

Library of Congress Control Number: 2009924630

Printed in the United States of America

iUniverse rev. date: 3/27/2009

# DEDICATION

For my family ... my five children and their spouses and the twelve amazing grandchildren who are my pride and my joy.

And for Jack Hekker (1931-2004) who turned my life around ... twice!

# Contents

PROLOGUE . . . . . . . . . . . . . . . . . . . . . . . . . . . . . . . . . . . . . . . . . . . . . xiii

CHAPTER 1 AFGO . . . . . . . . . . . . . . . . . . . . . . . . . . . . . . . . . . . . . . 1

CHAPTER 2 Don't Disregard Everything . . . . . . . . . . . . . . . . . . . . . 7

CHAPTER 3 Women's Changing Roles. . . . . . . . . . . . . . . . . . . . . . 13

CHAPTER 4 Wives and Mothers . . . . . . . . . . . . . . . . . . . . . . . . . . 19

CHAPTER 5 The Rella Cinder Syndrome. . . . . . . . . . . . . . . . . . . . 25

CHAPTER 6 The Madam was Adam. . . . . . . . . . . . . . . . . . . . . . . . 31

CHAPTER 7 Men and Why Women Love Them . . . . . . . . . . . . . . . 37

CHAPTER 8 Sex and the Possible. . . . . . . . . . . . . . . . . . . . . . . . . . 43

CHAPTER 9 Divorcees vs. Widows: The Dichotomy . . . . . . . . . . . . 49

CHAPTER 10 Divorce: Hell in the Hallway . . . . . . . . . . . . . . . . . . . 57

CHAPTER 11 Gedogen and Geezers. . . . . . . . . . . . . . . . . . . . . . . . . 63

CHAPTER 12 Divorce as a Tsunami. . . . . . . . . . . . . . . . . . . . . . . . . 69

CHAPTER 13 Send in the Clowns . . . . . . . . . . . . . . . . . . . . . . . . . . 75

CHAPTER 14 Age and the "Tiger" . . . . . . . . . . . . . . . . . . . . . . . . . . 81

CHAPTER 15 Marriage on the Rocks. . . . . . . . . . . . . . . . . . . . . . . . 89

CHAPTER 16 Men and Women: Need and Want. . . . . . . . . . . . . . . 95

CHAPTER 17 Bite Your Éclair . . . . . . . . . . . . . . . . . . . . . . . . . . . 101

CHAPTER 18 Evolution and Devolution . . . . . . . . . . . . . . . . . . . . 107

FINALE . . . . . . . . . . . . . . . . . . . . . . . . . . . . . . . . . . . . . . . . . . . 113

ACKNOWLEDGEMENTS. . . . . . . . . . . . . . . . . . . . . . . . . . . . . . . 115

BIOGRAPHY. . . . . . . . . . . . . . . . . . . . . . . . . . . . . . . . . . . . . . . 117

# Contents

# FOREWORD

When two *New York Times'* articles I'd written -- three decades apart -- came to define my married life, I confronted not only my own journey but a profound truth. That centuries from now, when the definitive history of the world is finally written, it will report that American women's lives changed forever in the second half of the twentieth century. On my watch!

Dr. Lionel Tiger, the Charles Darwin Professor of Anthropology at Rutgers University, observed that the result of the Women's Liberation Movement is that, "events have taken over the boldest expectations," and, "millions of years of evolutionary regularity have been altered in a very brief period."

Born into a society with long-established values and rules that changed midpoint in our lives, mine became the swing generation of women in that short timeframe whose adult years were defined by confusion and contradiction. So let's applaud the real heroines of the Women's Movement ... the transitional generation that survived all the turmoil. Not only did the rules change, the goal posts were moved and the playbook became obsolete. If our progeny were destined to be labeled Generation X, are women who came of age in the 1950s and '60s Generation Y-US?

The illustration on the next page accurately depicts the expectations of young wives in the 1950s and it was sent to me recently by a young woman friend with the note, "Isn't this hilarious?" The answer is, *"NO."*

*Housekeeping Monthly* 13 May 1955

*THE GOOD WIFE'S GUIDE, 1955*

- Have dinner ready. Plan ahead, even the night before, to have a delicious meal ready, on time for his return. This is a way of letting him know that you have been thinking about him and are concerned about his needs. Most men are hungry when they come home and the prospect of a good meal (especially his favourite dish) is part of the warm welcome needed.
- Prepare yourself. Take 15 minutes to rest so you'll be refreshed when he arrives. Touch up your make-up, put a ribbon in your hair and be fresh-looking. He has just been with a lot of work-weary people.
- Be a little gay and a little more interesting for him. His boring day may need a lift and one of your duties is to provide it.
- Clear away the clutter. Make one last trip through the main part of the house just before your husband arrives.
- Gather up schoolbooks, toys, paper etc and then run a dustcloth over the tables.
- Over the cooler months of the year you should prepare and light a fire for him to unwind by. Your husband will feel he has reached a haven of rest and order, and it will give you a lift too. After all, catering for his comfort will provide you with immense personal satisfaction.
- Prepare the children. Take a few minutes to wash the children's hands and faces (if they are small), comb their hair and, if necessary, change their clothes. They are little treasures and he would like to see them playing the part. Minimise all noise. At the time of his arrival, eliminate all noise of the washer, dryer or vacuum. Try to encourage the children to be quiet.
- Be happy to see him.
- Greet him with a warm smile and show sincerity in your desire to please him.
- Listen to him. You may have a dozen important things to tell him, but the moment of his arrival is not the time. Let him talk first – remember, his topics of conversation are more important than yours.
- Make the evening his. Never complain if he comes home late or goes out to dinner, or other places of entertainment without you. Instead, try to understand his world of strain and pressure and his very real need to be at home and relax.
- Your goal: Try to make sure your home is a place of peace, order and tranquility where your husband can renew himself in body and spirit.
- Don't greet him with complaints and problems.
- Don't complain if he's late home for dinner or even if he stays out all night. Count this as minor compared to what he might have gone through that day.
- Make him comfortable. Have him lean back in a comfortable chair or have him lie down in the bedroom. Have a cool or warm drink ready for him.
- Arrange his pillow and offer to take off his shoes. Speak in a low, soothing and pleasant voice.
- Don't ask him questions about his actions or question his judgment or integrity. Remember, he is the master of the house and as such will always exercise his will with fairness and truthfulness. You have no right to question him.
- A good wife always knows her place.

# PROLOGUE

*The New York Times*
Op-Ed Page, December 20, 1977
by Terry Martin Hekker

South Nyack, N. Y. – My son lied about it on his college application. My husband mutters it under his breath when asked. And I had grown reluctant to mention it myself.

The problem is my occupation. But the statistics on women that have come out since the Houston conference have given me a new outlook. I have ceased thinking of myself as obsolete and begun to see myself as I really am ... an endangered species. Like the whooping crane and the snow leopard, I deserve attentive nurturing and perhaps a distinctive metal tag on my foot. Because I am one of the last of a dying breed of human females designated, "Occupation: Housewife."

I know it's nothing to crow about. I realize that when people discuss their professions at parties I am more of a pariah than a hooker or a loan shark. I have been castigated, humiliated and scorned. In an age of do your own thing, it's clear no one meant me. I've been told (patiently and a little louder than necessary, as one does with a small child) that I am an anachronism (except that they avoid such a big word). I have been made to feel so outmoded that I wouldn't be surprised to discover that like a carton of yogurt, I have an expiration date stamped on my bottom.

I once treasured a small hope that history might vindicate me. After all, nursing was once just such a shameful occupation, suitable for only the lowest of women. But I abandoned any thought that my occupation would ever become fashionable again, just as I had to stop counting on full-figured women coming back into style. I'm a hundred years too late on both counts.

Now, however, thanks to all these new statistics, I see a brighter future for myself. Today, fewer than 16% of American families have a full-time, housewife-mother. Comparing that with previous figures, at the rate it's going I calculate I am less than eight years away from being the last housewife in the country. And then I intend to be impossible.

I shall demand enormous fees to go on talk shows, and charge for my autograph. Anthropologists will study my feeding and nesting habits through field glasses and keep notebooks detailing my every move. That is, if no one gets the bright idea that I'm so unique that I must be put behind sealed glass like the Book of Kells. In any event, I can expect to be a celebrity and to be pampered. I cannot, though, expect to get even.

There's no getting even for years of being regarded as stupid or lazy, or both. For years of being considered unproductive (unless you count five children which no one does). For years of being viewed as a parasite, living off a man (except by my husband whose opinion doesn't seem to matter). For years of fetching other women's children after they'd thrown up in the lunchroom, because I have nothing better to do, or probably there's nothing I do better, while their mothers have "careers." For years of caring for five children and a big house and constantly being asked when I'm going to work.

I come from a long line of women, most of them more Edith Bunker than Betty Freidan, who never knew they were unfulfilled. I can't testify that they were happy, but they were cheerful. And if they lacked "meaningful relationships," they cherished relations who meant something. They took pride in a clean, comfortable home and satisfaction in serving a good meal because no one had explained that the only work worth doing is that for which you get paid.

They enjoyed raising their children because no one ever told them that little children belonged in church basements and their mother belong somewhere else. They live very frugally on their husband's paychecks, because they didn't realize that it's more important to have a bigger house and a second car than it is to rear your own children. And they were so incredibly ignorant that they died never suspecting they'd been failures.

That won't hold true for me. I don't yet perceive myself as a failure, but it's not for want of being told I am. The other day, years of condescension prompted me to fib in order to test a theory. At a party where most of the guests were business associates of my husband, a Ms. Putdown asked me who I was. I told her I was Jack Hekker's wife. That had a galvanizing effect on her. She took my hand and asked if that was all I thought of myself…just someone's wife? I wasn't going to let her in on the five children, but when she persisted I mentioned them but told her that they weren't mine, that they belonged to my dead sister. And then I basked in the glow of her warm approval.

It's an absolute truth that whereas you are considered ignorant to stay home and raise your children, it is quite heroic to do so for someone else's children. Being a housekeeper is acceptable (even to the Social Security office) as long as it's not *your* house you're keeping. And treating a husband with attentive devotion is altogether correct as long as he's not *your* husband.

Sometimes I feel like Alice in Wonderland. But lately, mostly, I feel like an endangered species.

*Terry Martin Hekker has been married for 22 years. Her husband Jack M. Hekker is a lawyer and has been South Nyack's Village judge for 14 years.*

## THE END

*The New York Times,* January 1, 2006
Modern Love; Paradise Lost (Domestic Division)
by Terry Martin Hekker

A while back, at a baby shower for a niece, I overheard the expectant mother being asked if she intended to return to work after the baby was born. The answer, which rocked me, was, "Yes, because I don't want to end up like Aunt Terry."

That would be me.

In the continuing case of Full-Time Homemaker vs. Working Mother, I offer myself as Exhibit A. Because more than a quarter-century ago I wrote an Op-Ed article for *The New York Times* on the satisfaction of being a full-time housewife in the new age of the liberated woman. I wrote it from my heart, thoroughly convinced that homemaking and raising my children was the most challenging and rewarding job I could ever want.

"I come from a long line of women," I wrote, "most of them more Edith Bunker than Betty Freidan, who never knew they were unfulfilled. I can't testify that they were happy, but they were cheerful. ...They took pride in a clean, comfortable home and satisfaction in serving a good meal because no one had explained that the only work worth doing is that for which you get paid."

I wasn't advocating that mothers forgo careers to stay home with their children; I was simply defending my choice as a valid one. The mantra of the age may have been "Do your own thing," but as a full-time homemaker, that didn't seem to mean me.

The column morphed into a book titled, "Ever Since Adam and Eve," followed by a national tour on which I, however briefly, became the authority on homemaking as a viable choice for women. I ultimately told my story on "Today" and to Dinah Shore, Charlie Rose and even to Oprah, when she was the host of a local TV show in Baltimore.

In subsequent years I lectured on the rewards of homemaking and housewifery. While others tried to make the case that women like me were parasites and little more than legalized prostitutes, I spoke to rapt audiences about the importance of being there for your children as they grew up, of the satisfactions of "making a home," preparing family meals and supporting your hard-working husband.

So I was predictably stunned and devastated when, on our 40th wedding anniversary, my husband presented me with a divorce. I knew our first anniversary would be paper, but never expected the 40th would be papers, 16 of them meticulously detailing my faults and flaws, the reason our marriage, according to him, was over.

We had been married by a bishop with a blessing from the pope in a country church filled with honeysuckle and hope. Five children and six grandchildren later we were divorced by a third-rate judge in a suburban courthouse reeking of dust and despair.

Our long marriage had its full share of love, complications, illnesses, joy and stress. Near the end we were in a dismal period, with my husband in treatment for alcoholism. And although I had made more than my share of mistakes, I never expected to be served with divorce papers. I was stunned to find myself, at this stage of life, marooned. And it was small comfort that I wasn't alone. There were many other confused women of my age and circumstance who'd been married just as long, sharing my situation.

I was in my teens when I first read Dickens' "*Great Expectations*" with the tale of Miss Haversham, who, stood up by her groom-to-be, spent decades in her yellowing wedding gown, sitting at her cobweb-covered bridal banquet table, consumed with plotting revenge. I felt then that to be left waiting at the altar with a church full of people must be the most crushing thing that could happen to a woman.

I was wrong. No jilted bride could feel as embarrassed and humiliated as a woman in her sixties discarded by her husband. I was confused and scared, and the pain of being tossed aside by the love of my life made bitterness unavoidable. In those first few bewildering months, as I staggered and wailed though my life, I made Miss Haversham look like a good sport.

Sitting around my kitchen with two friends who had also been dumped by their husbands, I figured out that among the three of us we'd been married 110 years. We'd been faithful wives, good mothers, cooks and housekeepers who'd married in the '50s, when "dress for success" meant a wedding gown and "wife" was a tenured position.

Turns out we had a lot in common with our outdated kitchen appliances. Like them we were serviceable, low maintenance, front-loading, self-cleaning and (relatively) frost-free. Also like them we had warranties that had run out. Our husbands sought sleeker models with features we lacked who could execute tasks we'd either never learned or couldn't perform without laughing.

Like most loyal wives of our generation, we'd contemplated eventual widowhood but never thought we'd end up divorced. And "divorced" doesn't begin to describe the pain of this process. "Canceled" is more like it. It began with my credit cards, then my health insurance and checkbook, until, finally, like a used postage stamp, I felt canceled too.

I faced frightening losses and was overwhelmed by the injustice of it all. He got to take his girlfriend to Cancun, while I got to sell my engagement ring to pay the roofer. When I filed my first nonjoint tax return, it triggered the shocking notification that I had become eligible for food stamps.

The judge had awarded me alimony that was less than I was used to getting for household expenses, and now I had to use that money to pay bills I'd never seen before: mortgage, taxes, insurance and car payments. And that princely sum was awarded for only four years, the judge suggesting that I go for job training when I turned 67. Not only was I unprepared for divorce itself, I was utterly lacking in skills to deal with the brutal aftermath.

I read about the young mothers of today - educated, employed, self-sufficient - who drop out of the work force when they have children, and I worry and wonder. Perhaps it is the right choice for them. Maybe they'll be fine. But the fragility of modern marriage suggests that at least half of them may not be.

Regrettably, women whose husbands are devoted to their families and are good providers must nevertheless face the specter of future abandonment. Surely the seeds of this wariness must have been planted, even if they can't believe it could ever happen to them. Many have witnessed their own mothers jettisoned by their own fathers and seen divorced friends trying to rear children with marginal financial and emotional support.

These young mothers are often torn between wanting to be home with their children and the statistical possibility of future calamity, aware that one of the most poverty-stricken groups in today's society are divorced older women. The feminine and sexual revolutions of the last few decades have had their shining victories, but have they, in the end, made things any easier for mothers?

I cringe when I think of that line from my Op-Ed article about the long line of women I'd come from and belonged to who were able to find fulfillment as homemakers "because no one had explained" to us "that the only work worth doing is that for which you get paid." For a divorced mother, the harsh reality is that the work for which you do get paid is the only work that will keep you afloat.

These days, couples face complex negotiations over work, family, childcare and housekeeping. I see my children dealing with these issues in their marriages, and I understand the stresses and frustrations. It becomes evident that where traditional marriage through the centuries had been a partnership based on mutual dependency, modern marriage demands greater self-sufficiency.

While today's young women know from the start they'll face thorny decisions regarding careers, marriage and children, those of us who married in the 50's anticipated lives similar to our mothers' and grandmothers'. Then we watched with bewilderment as all the rules changed, and the goal posts were moved.

If I had it to do over again, I'd still marry the man I married and have my children: they are my treasure and a powerful support system for me and for one another. But I would have used the years after my youngest started school to further my education. I could have amassed two doctorates using the time and energy I gave to charitable and community causes and been better able to support myself.

But in a lucky twist, my community involvement had resulted in my being appointed to fill a vacancy on our Village Board. I had been serving as titular deputy mayor of my hometown (Nyack, N.Y.) when my husband left me. Several weeks later the mayor chose not to run again because of failing health, and I was elected to succeed him, becoming the first female mayor.

I held office for six years, a challenging, full-time job that paid a whopping annual salary of $8,000. But it consumed me and gave me someplace to go every day and most nights, and as such it saved my sanity. Now, mostly retired except for some part-time work, I am kept on my toes by 12 amazing grandchildren.

My anachronistic book was written while I was in a successful marriage that I expected would go on forever. Sadly, it now has little relevance for modern women, except perhaps as a cautionary tale: never its intended purpose. So I couldn't imagine writing a sequel. But my friend Elaine did come up with a perfect title: "Disregard First Book."

*Terry Martin Hekker is a writer in Nyack, N.Y.*

# CHAPTER 1

# AFGO

My original *New York Times'* Op-Ed column had gone around the world on their news service and the response was overwhelming, because I had touched on a problem, a prejudice, which hundreds of women thought they were facing alone. And now, almost thirty years later, the issue is still hot and dubbed, "The Mommy Wars," indicating the perceived hostility between working and stay-at-home mothers.

But it was my absolute faith in my husband and our marriage that I trumpeted back then, which led to my almost fatal collapse when faced with divorce. I had dedicated *Ever Since Adam and Eve* to my inspirations ... my mother and grandmother. And in some sort of cosmic prescience, I had a note further down the page:

*"I considered dedicating this to my husband until I noticed how many women dedicated first books to their supportive and understanding husbands who subsequently decided to support and understand a younger women. Why tempt the fates?"*

Why indeed and why did I ever think that was funny? And how could my great marriage end so badly when it began so hopefully? In the mid-fifties, I was just out of college and working in my father's business. At a party in the Statler Hotel in Manhattan, a tall, handsome Marine lieutenant came though the door. I turned to my friend Janet and said I'd better find out his name because I was going to marry him. I was absolutely certain. Jack didn't have a clue. I pursued him shamelessly and the first time I brought him home for dinner my oldest brother said, "Nice to meet you. Do you have a brother? Because if you don't I could be the best man." He knew. They all knew. It was clear from

1

the beginning this marriage was meant to be. My Irish grandmother proclaimed, "God made them and matched them."

Weeks later when Jack asked my father if we could be married next Christmas, the response was, "What the hell's the matter with Thanksgiving?" My father said his sense of urgency was precipitated by the fact that I was looking at the guy like a starving man looks at a plate of spaghetti.

We had an extravagant wedding, Jack graduated from Georgetown Law School, we bought a drafty Victorian house in the lower Hudson Valley and he opened a law office a few blocks away. Our five children flourished in this Norman Rockwell please-don't-eat-the-daisies environment. If a fortune-teller had told me back then that I'd end my life divorced, I'd have called her a quack and demanded my money back.

I never, ever thought I'd be divorced and still have trouble accepting it. Faced with a form that lists "single," "divorced," "widowed," I check them all. Basically I hate the word "divorced." What I'd prefer is "retired" which has a connotation of years of loyal service followed by an honorable discharge from active duty. In the confusion about how I should now sign my name ... back to my maiden name ... hyphenated maiden/married name? Could I sign "Mrs. John M. Hekker (Ret.)" like those pompous old colonels in Agatha Christie stories? In those first terrible years, that might have allowed me one small shred of dignity.

Each divorce, like each marriage, is unique and you can drive yourself nuts trying to figure out what went wrong and when. But however varied the causes of long-term marriages breaking up, I became aware of a strong commonality in the consequences. And oddly enough for someone who fancies herself a rather highbrow reader, back then when the wounds were raw, I discovered that commonality not in the serious tomes on divorce but in the tasty murder mysteries that became escape devices in my new empty-bedtime reading.

My personal favorite, Susan Isaacs, began her book, *After All These Years*, with, "After nearly a quarter of a century of marriage, Richie Meyers, my husband, told me to call him 'Rick.' Then he started slicking back his hair {so} how come I was surprised when Richie told me he was leaving me for ... Jessica."

Sharyn McCrumb took as the title of her mystery a phrase overheard from a battered woman, *If I'd Killed Him When I Met Him I'd Be Out of Jail By Now*. It's the story of a dumped wife who snaps and murders her ex-husband and his bitch (Golden Retriever) of a new wife. The unrepentant murderess suggests that middle-aged men get strange. "I think it's testosterone poisoning. Do you suppose anyone's working on a cure? We could organize a telethon …! Poor Baldy is doomed to a life of bimbos and Nordic Track unless you help." Her rage fueled by the "cosmic double standard … the fact that men get more than one chance to live happily ever after."

In her witty novel, *Murdering Mr. Monte*, the brilliant Judith Viorst describes a meeting of a group of wives in their fifties and sixties who'd been deserted by their husbands. "Urged by their counselors … to regard their new unattached status not as a loss but a chance to grow," they call their support group "AFGO"… as in my husband walks out and gets a sexy new girlfriend and I get A̲nother F̲**king G̲rowth O̲pportunity."

That one rang a loud bell. 'AFGO' became my mantra. It's my license plate. Because I've seen it over and over. A former (not firmer) wife struggling to put a positive spin on a crushing progression of terrifying events. His income doubles while hers is halved. She struggles to "carpe diem" while he "carpes" a redhead. And the judge's idea of equitable distribution is that he gets the Buick and she gets the salad shooter. AFGO!

In the hectic roller-coaster years since my first, and only, book, I didn't have the heart, literally, to write about anything but I had time to consider and ponder and recognize the changing face of marriage and the whole man/woman thing and relationships and children. Acknowledging that women's roles are no longer an oscillating swing of mores, but a steep and slippery slope pitched away from housewifery.

I have come to appreciate that my most personal angst reflects the profound shift in women's lives and is not specific to me but is part of a larger, more significant dynamic, one that drastically changed the entire social order. And that change which appears as a catastrophe can instead force growth, because every ending, however heartbreaking, forces a new beginning.

So a few years ago, I wrote a book called "Occupation Housewife" about my journey from dumped housefrau to joyful and independent woman. A dozen editors turned it down. They tried to be kind, flattering my quirky writing style and most loved my voice (whatever that means). But *no* takers because they saw *no* interest in my subject and absolutely *no* possibility for any media coverage.

I was devastated. Several years of my life wasted at a time when I could least afford missing years. So I thought maybe if I just wrote an article about being divorced after a long marriage and sent it to my morning paper, *The New York Times*, it might resonate with a small pool of readers. I hit a geyser. Within hours of its publication, *The Today Show* called to book an interview with Katie Couric, who was gracious and encouraging and said goodbye with, "write that book!"

The U.K. papers sent a photographer for pictures to run with columns in the *Manchester Guardian* and *London Times*. BBC called repeatedly for phone interviews and NPR invited me to do an hour call-in program. Reporters called from Dublin, Paris and Wales. A sympathetic interviewer wrote a major piece for *El Mercurio* in Chile and another cried for me in Argentina. I was part of a panel hosted by Diane Sawyer on *Good Morning America* and asked to do a "salon" with the editorial staff at *Cosmopolitan*, which ran my column in their June '06 issue. And to top it off, the popular Irish folk singer Eleanor McAvoy transformed it into lyrics for her hit song, *Old New Borrowed Blue*. It's quite a trip hearing your most personal feelings rhymed and sung.

It wasn't all sunshine and roses. I received several negative emails (mostly from men) and often my story was used in books by other women to reaffirm ideas that clashed with mine. And it didn't stop there. For a small fee, I gave the textbook publisher, Longman Publishing Group, permission to use my two *Times'* articles in a book on essay writing called *Writing and Reading Across the Curriculum*. I was flattered that I would be the only writer represented by two essays. Well, when they sent me the finished book there were notes after my essays on subjects a teacher might want to explore. One was, "to what extent do you feel that the self-confident Hekker got her comeuppance? To what extent do you feel she deserves your sympathy and support? On a blog site in response to the 2006 column, one poster criticized Hekker as

4

self-pitying and bitter. Do you agree with this assessment? Describe your own reaction upon reading the paragraph beginning, 'So I was predictably stunned and devastated when, on our fortieth wedding anniversary, my husband presented me with a divorce.'" Interesting! I'd like to know how those student responses went. Or maybe I wouldn't.

But the heartwarming part about the larger journey I've been on these last few years came from the letters — hundreds of them — sent by the gutsy women who faced similar situations or hoped to avoid them, and saw their experiences reflected in mine. Some of the letters were pages long, stories that could be movies of the week on *Lifetime*. And it is with their encouragement that I rewrote that unsold manuscript to reflect historical (and hysterical) stages in the evolution of women, reflected in my friend Elaine's admonition to, *Disregard First Book.*

# CHAPTER 2
## Don't Disregard Everything

I almost didn't use the title, *Disregard First Book,* because basically I still accept as true most of the precepts of that first book. I believe that family is the bedrock of civilization and I believe in marriage. I loved being married with every joy doubled and every sorrow halved. It always made me smile when couples said, "we're not getting married, we're just living together." Because getting married is fun … it's the living together that's tough.

My decades as a homemaker and mother were the very best years of my life. The most rewarding. The most joyful. I never worked so hard and never was happier, notwithstanding that I found that the sleep-depriving care of infants most challenging -- a lot like deep sea fishing -- hours of tedium punctuated by minutes of panic. For over thirty years I lived in a comfortable home surrounded by the people I loved most. As each of the children left for college it was like a death in the family. I missed them so much. But by the time they came home for Thanksgiving I wondered how I'd ever managed the confusion and chaos.

When they were all gone our big drafty home was more than empty … it was hollow. A house that once held so much life and laughter seemed haunted. So we sold it and moved to a spacious apartment about ten blocks away. My life changed direction but it didn't change course. It remained centered around my husband, my children and their businesses, while my husband, who'd often worked sixty hours a week to support us all, found time to pursue his passion for golf and other amusements. Our marriage hit a new level, which I thought was appropriate and rewarding. God was I wrong.

With the tuition bills behind us, we traveled and dined out more and absorbed the finer points of good wine. And Jack was finally able to join a first-rate golf club where it is de rigueur to start drinking at noon. It took a few years but my formerly teetotaler husband was transformed from an occasional social drinker into a full-blown alcoholic.

Jack and I kidded about being kept together for decades by a "cheap physical attraction" but there was truth in that. Our king-size, four-poster bed was roomy but we always slept with toes touching. We shared adventures big and small. We used to fly to Europe, rent a car and go exploring ... two for the road. We stomped at the Savoy, jitterbugged in the Piazza San Marco and waltzed across the upper deck of a ship sailing through the Dardanelles. We made love in dozens of romantic chateaus and inns and in the Gresham Hotel in Dublin, in the Paris Hotel in Monte Carlo and in an obscure box at the Old Vic during an even more obscure Pinter play. We loved and laughed. A lot. I absolutely never ever thought we could end up divorced when we had such a good thing going. Going. Gone.

It took about five years for our marriage to collapse under alcohol's corrosive force. As alcoholism took its cruel hold on Jack, my life became a rollercoaster of hope and despair. Every dreadful event engendered vows to never drink again. But those earnest vows were always broken and it inevitably followed that marriage vows also got fractured. Which I felt, then and now, was not about sex, but about being validated and valued by admiring women who were unaffected by the brutal downward spiral alcohol inflicted on my big, handsome, charming and ill-fated husband.

When an attractive older man (or even an ugly one) leaves his wife, there is no shortage of women out there ready to welcome him with open arms (and legs). Ultimately our marriage was put asunder not as much by alcohol, but by a series of aging debutantes who seized the opportunity to grab a troubled man ... mine.

I had trouble forgiving those tootsies and eventually so did Jack -- all those romances ended badly. One of them exploded into the tabloids. Booze tore him from me, but it was those opportunistic women who validated and fueled his post-alcoholic anger that kept him from returning home after he achieved sobriety. One actually called me to apologize, saying he was a rudderless ship without his family and me, and she regretted hurting us. Happily, after years of bouncing around, Jack finally came to his senses and shortly before he died, he married a good, kind woman who cared for him.

My husband left me on my sixty-first birthday. The actual divorce came two years later on our fortieth wedding anniversary. The man had a real sense of "occasion." So I have lived alone for over fifteen years and I did not even begin this book until a few years ago, when, given the fact that all survival is temporary, I knew I had triumphed over the horribly painful consequences of divorce.

The day those unanticipated papers were served on me was apocalyptic. My first thought was how painful this would be for our children. And then it hit me like lightning that I would be spending the rest of my days living alone and I became terrified. My heart was pounding as I began to process swirling emotions. I felt mortified. Humiliated. Frightened. But oddly enough I never felt lonely, and eventually the overwhelming feeling of abandonment gave way to the sensation of freedom. And I slowly discovered coping mechanisms, and can honestly say I have a better life than I ever could have imagined back then. Except for the hurt the divorce caused our children and the confusion it's caused our grandchildren, both of us actually had better lives. Certainly my husband did, even given his rather rocky love life. But at least he *had* a love life.

Because of my involvement with community projects, I had been appointed to our village board as a trustee and then deputy mayor. But weeks after Jack left, when the mayor of our village had stepped down due to ill health, I went from two nights a month meetings as a trustee, to the full-time job of mayor. It was my salvation. It numbed the pain to have a place to go every day and most nights. I felt totally unprepared to be a mayor until I realized the best possible training was having been married to an alcoholic. I was used to being blamed for everything. But now I was getting paid for it (a princely $8,000 a year).

I served three terms as the first woman mayor of Nyack, and there was a steep learning curve, but I made new friends as I clutched the old ones. When I chose not to run again, I accepted a low paying but fun job doing special projects and community outreach for our local Equity theater.

Because I now live above a store in the downtown and have some empty rooms, I made those rooms available to actors working at the theater. I've had adventures and gotten to know people I'd never been closer to than orchestra seats. The best was Julie Harris, one of the finest actresses who ever lived and whose continued friendship I treasure. Almost every night after her show, *The Belle of Amherst*, the director Charles Nelson Reilly would call, and if we weren't home yet, he'd leave messages accusing us of cruising bars to pick up sailors.

I shared catalogues with Sandy Duncan and shopped with Loretta Swit. Rich Little proved to be the most gentle of men but there are a few I won't mention on the advice of counsel. One famous singer-actress took advantage of my being out of town to fill my apartment with her relatives and then complained about the stock of fresh towels.

When the theater downsized, I was laid off (why is being laid so much more fun than being laid off). In any event I found myself, age sixty-nine, in a long line of frightened people at the unemployment office. And oddly enough, my sense of failure centered around how disappointed my parents must be in me ... the daughter they so loved and educated and left with such high hopes. I felt I'd let them down but became even more determined to overcome the misfortunes that seemed to dog me. I refused to die as the poor relation.

So it may have been a bumpy journey but I have achieved recovery and peace. Most of the women who wrote to me are still in the process of reinventing fractured lives and each one seems to have handled things differently. One wrote a long letter about her husband leaving her for his girlfriend after a thirty-five year marriage. When she realized the television in her husband's den had been a gift from the girlfriend, she took it, along with a large ax, out into the yard. She sent along a picture of herself, ax raised above her head, and another showing the 8,256 pieces of what had been a large Sony TV. She claimed it helped.

Another woman wrote about her husband bailing out of a long marriage and the judge awarding her minimal support, even though a criminal trial proved he'd squirreled away millions embezzled from his company. It was small comfort that he was spending five years in a federal prison ... but it *was* a comfort. She's writing a book.

It wasn't just the abandoned wives who contacted me. One younger woman wrote of the pain she'd felt when her father disappeared from her wedding reception never to return to her astonished mother. In fact, many letters were from the children of brutal divorces whose lives were rocked by their parents' divorces.

One lovely mother of five wrote about being abandoned by her husband after twenty-five years, and confessed that given her limited options, she might found an order of nuns to be called, "Little Sisters of the Dumped."

The most upbeat letter came from a divorced older woman who discovered that her ex was planning an intimate but elegant wedding to his young girlfriend at a nearby posh resort. She selected the most garish invitations -- multi-colored with doves, ribbons and flowers -- and just before the event sent a hundred of them to his colleagues inviting them to the wedding with the admonishment, "No RSVP Required – Just Join Us On This Happy Day." That marriage lasted only a little longer than the wedding reception itself and both proved terribly expensive. *The First Wives' Club* notwithstanding, deserted wives don't always get the last laugh but when they do, oh my do we celebrate.

# CHAPTER 3
## Women's Changing Roles

When I was growing up, divorce was unheard of in long-term marriages and any man who bailed out on his children's mother would have been ostracized. Men were usually awarded some slack regarding infidelity, but families were sacred and breaking them up was dishonorable. But that was in the halcyon days before selfishness became socially acceptable.

It was the flourishing women's movement that altered everything for us wives of the fifties and sixties, and I can't believe I didn't see it coming. After all a prime catalyst lived on my street ... a half-mile south but the *same* street. We even shared a grocer who delivered to my little apartment over a garage on his way to her grand Victorian house. I needed food delivered because I had four children under five and no car, and she needed them because she was busy writing a book. John, the deliveryman, used to tell me about her (he said I was a better housekeeper).

Her name was Betty Freidan and the book was *The Feminine Mystique,* and it made her the Mother of the Women's Movement. But, no disrespect to Ms. Freidan, the birth control pill and the ensuing sexual revolution also had a great impact on altering the lives of women. All these forces merged with the colossal force intrinsic to an idea whose time had come.

In her landmark book, *I Don't Know How She Does It,* Allison Pearson's heroine explains to a female colleague, "... there was all history and then there was us. There's never been anything like us before ... Century after century of women knowing their place and suddenly it's twenty years of women who don't know their place and it's scary for men. It's happened too fast."

Women's Liberation with its demands for equality was long overdue. But like all revolutions, it required some refining. Because, as with most social movements, its leaders didn't fully appreciate the unintended consequences, like the impact on family structure and the corresponding liberation of men. Which ultimately socked me in the solar plexus because it resulted in the now well-documented license it gave older men to leave their wives with almost no societal consequences. What's good for the goose can be even better for the gander.

The realignment of social structure and accelerating divorce rate had an unfortunate outcome in that, today, even young mothers with husbands who are devoted to their families and are good providers, must recognize the 50-50 possibility of future abandonment.

It isn't enough to have a good education because if you're out of today's shifting job market for too long, it's tricky to jump back in. And, coming full circle from my first book, having eaten several crows, I would tell every young mother who wants to stay home with her children that it's a marvelous experience (and one I will never regret) but she should keep an eye on the employment market. It's a kind of insurance she may never need but she'll never regret having.

A young attorney contemplating motherhood, called in to me on the NPR radio talk show to say she had changed her focus from trial work to estate planning, because it would be more compatible with working from her home. That seemed an enlightened approach. One young mother told me she had decided to study dentistry -- cosmetic dentistry -- because she could have a solid profession with a home office and regular hours. So it seems more and more young women who plan on having children are thinking ahead to make career decisions compatible with family life.

Also many working parents have recognized the advantage of living closer to their families who can provide a safety net in their high-wire lives. It fills my life and my heart that the working mothers in my family call on me for emergency services. I can collect a sick grandchild from school, and when a child is too ill to go to school, he or she can be dropped off at grandma's house. My guestroom bed has a teddy bear as a permanent resident. The stresses endemic to two working parents have made the supportive extended family unit even more precious.

You know those good news/bad news jokes? Well it took me seventy years to figure out the real joke -- that the good news and the bad news are frequently the same news. Each good thing that happens has a down side. Things that have a ghastly beginning end up blessings in disguise (and haven't we all had our fill of them?). Graduation, marriage, new baby, promotion, retirement all require congratulations - and condolences. Because each brings its own duties and responsibilities. Worse yet, disasters often begin brilliantly disguised as opportunities.

A superlative example of this theorem is this dichotomy of Women's Liberation, which has offered us girls' options and problems that our grandmothers never imagined. So our lives are better *and* worse. Our opportunities are greater, ditto our obligations. We are the first generation of women in the history of Planet Earth who are generally expected to have babies, care for a home and work outside it. Bring home the bacon and then cook it. If these are exceptional times for women, they are also hazardous, because today's females are pioneers navigating uncharted waters. And here be dragons.

When I was born, the first grandchild in two large Irish families, no one looked down into my crib and said, "someday she'll be President." Or, "the way she yammers she'll make a great lawyer." The highest hope held out for me was that I'd make a good marriage. And my situation was the norm. Despite grades that would have ushered me into almost any university, my parents sent me to study Home Economics with the nuns and I was contented with that choice. No girl I knew wanted a career. When we went off to college it was to prepare us for "just in case" jobs like teaching and nursing. Something to turn to in case we picked lemons in the garden of love (where they say only peaches grow!).

So when we married in the fifties, we envisioned lives much like our mothers. We accepted the role that the 1955 magazine delineated, and if you need further proof, watch the reruns of *Leave It To Beaver* and notice June Cleaver cleaning her house wearing pearls. But cropping up in quick succession was Women's Lib and the population explosion. Both fueled by the pill. From birth we'd been told to aim at being good wives and mothers. We should be content to remain supporting players in our own lives … our husbands took the leads. But almost overnight, having many children flipped from being noble to being selfish.

Being supported by a husband ceased to be honorable, and for the first time in history, married women with careers became the rule rather than the exception. By the mid-seventies, I found myself with a husband, five children, a big old drafty house and people asking me when I was going to go to work. I hung in there but recognized what Aunt Adelaide called "the handwriting in the hall."

Everything changed. We became so liberated from our traditional roles that we weren't even called women any more. We became "persons." Chairpersons. Salespersons. A particularly strident feminist referred to her lady mail carrier as a "person person." We started dressing like men in dark suits and stopped padding our bras and began padding our shoulders. It was a dizzying time to be a woman. Especially this woman. Besides the changing mores, we had to cope with one depression, five recessions, four wars, the Cuban missile crisis, the energy crisis and mid-life crisis (person-o-pause). The changes were disturbing but the worst was yet to come. The sexual revolution.

Fathers saw the sexual revolution appear just as they were running low on ammunition. And mothers who never knew unmarried sex watched their children's open lifestyles with awe and envy. Back in the 1950s, when you had a yen for a guy, the choices were marriage or living in sin which was guaranteed to send you to hell and kill your mother. In those days "safe sex" meant you were married and women yearned for sex without babies. And never imagined wanting babies without sex.

Now our daughters are the first generation in this culture who can have sexual relations outside marriage without being stigmatized or ostracized. And about time, since men never had those constraints. Trouble is sex was more fun when it was forbidden. At least it was more romantic. Couples today don't have romances, they have relationships. Romances (aka affairs) involved sharing four-poster beds in country inns and splits of champagne, while relationships involve sharing the laundry and splitting the rent. Relationships require incessant scrutiny, reassessing, and evaluation.

In my day we didn't have relationships. When you met a guy you wanted to "go all the way" with, you had to marry him before you jumped into bed with him. By the time you realized he was a jerk and he realized you were boring, you had three kids and a mortgage and made the best of it. And thirty years later, as you climb the stairs to your bedroom and he says he wants to go all the way tonight, he probably means he's going to turn the electric blanket on high.

# CHAPTER 4
## Wives and Mothers

The question is, are modern couples who worked through their sexual relationships going to have better marriages than those of us whose wedding nights were best described as the original amateur hour? And in a time when it was proffered that Niagara Falls was the second biggest disappointment in a young bride's life. If you use the divorce rate as a barometer here, the answer is no. But us women in the 'Y-US?' generation got the worst deal of all ... virginal weddings that ended in divorce decades later as men began feeling entitled to their liberation. Free to dump older wives for what they consider their just desserts ... tarts, strudel, cupcakes.

Younger men have also switched their strategies. In her brilliant book, *Are Men Necessary?*, Maureen Dowd quotes a male friend as saying that, "Deep down beneath the bluster and machismo, men are simply afraid to say that what they're truly looking for in a woman is an intelligent, confident and dependable partner in life whom they can devote themselves to unconditionally until she's forty."

It's not all bad news. The good news is that women today are sexually and economically more equal to men and have found acceptance in universities and the professions, business and politics with opportunities undreamt of less than six decades ago. As wives and mothers, they are not locked into full-time isolated care of their children. Better educated than their own mothers and grandmothers, they will probably work harder and experience more stress.

My grandmother O'Donohue had seven children and her fireman husband provided for them. Her only laborsaving devices were a washing machine with a wringer, a vacuum cleaner and an electric mixer with two speeds — on and off. And every afternoon she took a nap. I don't know one modern mother, with her panoply of laborsaving appliances, who can manage that.

My mother lived the same life as grandma, albeit with better appliances and working conditions. My daughter is living a life that is totally different and there's no going back. And what this deregulation of traditional mores really boils down to is choices. My generation and those women before me were lucky to get one from column A and one from column B, while my daughter's peers have selections like the menu in a Greek diner.

Often on that long-ago book tour I was asked if, given my new 'celebrity' status, would I ever be content to return to being just-a-housewife? The truth was I became even more convinced that I'd taken the right road. That my happiness and fulfillment were inexorably tied to my husband, our children and our home. I loved being a housewife even if perceived to be "a dinosaur surviving the crunch."

For a middle-aged New Yorker who'd never been further west than Philadelphia, that book tour had been a thrilling adventure. But by the time I returned home three weeks later, my bowels were in knots, my nerves were in shreds and my luggage was in Tulsa. My youngest son had taped a note to my bedroom mirror that read, "welcum home. I mist you."

I was being courted to write a newspaper column -- a poor man's Erma Bombeck -- but I had the nagging feeling that my marriage might not survive if I chose a "career." That I'd better not "Begin the Beguine." My husband, like most men in those days, expected to be the number one priority in his wife's life. Even when I was away from home for a couple of days on the lecture circuit, I sensed he felt abandoned and resentful, so this was not a difficult choice for me, because I deeply loved my husband and cherished our life together.

Decades later, I had cause to regret that decision, but for almost thirty-five years, I had a glorious and happy life with a man I truly loved, so if, eventually, I paid a price I couldn't afford, in retrospect I was more fortunate than most. I'd be an ingrate not to recognize that for decades I'd had a loving husband who gave me incredible fulfillment and support.

In fact, back when the publisher demanded a book tour, I insisted that my husband come along. We'd never been separated and I needed his strength and backup. Our lucky break was having his parents willing to watch the children for three weeks. My father-in-law was a lovely man and I had an incredible mother-in-law, who for the most part, never thought I was quite good enough for her son. Nothing I did or accomplished changed her mind very much, although on her deathbed she sent for me. She had to tell me something important. It was, "I know he's my son and you're my daughter-in-law, but I have to tell you. These Hekker men are grand-looking fellas, but cheaper men never drew life from God. So when the time comes get your Social Security check in your own name." How *did* she know?

Whatever her misgivings about me, she was a devoted grandmother to my children and she and gramps kept the home fires burning. Literally. She arrived clutching her stovetop potato baker which she used daily to magically transform large Idaho potatoes into small chunks of charcoal. Her specialty was "hamburger surprise," the surprise being that she wrapped chopped meat around a hard-boiled egg before over-cooking it. Frequently the real surprise was the crunchiness supplied by bits of eggshell. She was, hands down, the worst cook I've ever known.

With my book published, she grudgingly assured me that I had become a success. I was curious about her idea of success and she explained, "you'll probably get a picture with your obituary." That seemed a trifle hollow so I pressed on, trying to impress her by carefully going over the book tour itinerary, which included the best hotels in every city -- the Beverly Hills, the Fairmount, The Ritz Carlton, etc. Every night a new hotel and every day beginning with an appearance on the local morning TV show. I said, "Isn't it exciting?" She shot back, "you're going to be awfully constipated." Her clairvoyance kind of made up for the cooking.

She was long gone when her son divorced me, but gramps remained kind and gentle, and continued to go on vacation with the children and me. It was painful and confusing for him as divorce can be for any grandparent witnessing the wrenching apart of his family.

In those first horrible months alone, especially around him, I tried to disguise my hurt but I have never felt more miserable, more defeated, more sorrowful. Then one night I went to a concert version of the *Abba* musical, *Chess,* and unexpectedly, I began to cry listening to the Tim Rice lyrics:

*"Wasn't it good? Wasn't he fine?*
*Isn't it madness he won't be mine?"*

That was followed by, *Heaven Help My Heart*, which touched another raw nerve, and I began to literally sob my heart out, bewildering people around me. But there was a catharsis in those tears and soon after that I began recovering. The thing is like many of the women who responded to the *Modern Love* column, I couldn't stop loving my husband. The habits of a lifetime, the conditioned responses, the power of shared memories flooded back one Saturday morning in March, when I got a call from a woman thousands of miles away who'd been sent my column by a friend. Her husband of forty-five years just walked out and she was devastated. I could hardly understand what she was saying because she cried so.

She told me she was preparing an eight-page letter to her husband enumerating all the sacrifices she'd made for him, and just how ungrateful he had been for the last several years. She was making copies for her children. He wanted a divorce but she'll fight it because they once had such a good marriage. She needed someone to commiserate with and also give advice.

I am totally unqualified to give counsel. But what I could offer was the guidance I'd been given by my friend Connie who is also a first-rate therapist -- suggestions I credit with getting me through the worst times and which yielded positive results. She told me that when I felt hurt -- the stories that usually began, "you won't believe what he did now" -- I should tell *her.* Period. Don't share the information with my children because that man is their father. Don't burden my family and friends who may already feel uncomfortable due to divided loyalties. She suggested that when asked about my husband's leaving, I should answer that he seems to be a troubled man and then change the subject. I learned that you'll never regret taking the high road, which may even get you where you want to be faster. I begged the caller to think carefully before sending those letters.

On the subject of divorce itself, which I find devastating when children are involved, I had no choice. My husband was divorcing me. A good friend, understanding my quandary, paid for me to have a session with a world-famous (and very expensive) therapist in Manhattan, 'Dr. F'. The man barely looked at me, just took notes as he asked questions about my marriage, my husband's behavior, my reactions, etc. After almost an hour of insightful questions, he looked up at me and asked, "Is that your red coat on that chair by the door?" It was. He told me to put it on and get my own lawyer to hasten, not deflect, a divorce. Because that man I loved and with whom I shared the happiest days of my life was gone and was never coming back and I must create a new life for myself. As I left he said, "when you've worked through this terrible time you're going to be happy. On your own you can be someone." It struck me as an oddly inappropriate conclusion to our session, and I was grateful I wasn't paying him.

But it stuck with me and came flooding back several years later. A neighbor from my old life, the Broadway legend Elaine Stritch, (she of the "disregard" line) had been a constant support. Newly widowed herself, she was an inspiration, and took me to my first Al-Anon meeting, and began including me in her life, to the extent that I sometimes traveled with her when she gave concerts or did a movie on location.

Elaine had a wildly successful one-woman Broadway show, and took it to London, and I returned with her to the Savoy Hotel. Posh! We were joined there by her friends Marc Rosen and his wife, the remarkable Arlene Dahl, who is as bright and kind as she is beautiful. Arlene had a personal appearance at a prestigious English charity event celebrating the glory days of the MGM musicals, and the producer sent a vintage Rolls Royce for all of us.

Now, I live in a two-story walkup over a store, and drove a twelve-year-old vintage Saturn, so between the Rolls and the Savoy I was in heaven. The suggested dress was "Hollywood Glitz" and I finally got to put on a velvet jacket with feathers I'd bought in balmier days and had never worn, with blinding rhinestone earrings designed by Elaine's friend Donald Stannard. We arrived at the event, exited the Rolls onto a red carpet and found ourselves in the company of two other honorees -- Patricia Neal and Betty Garrett. A very young reporter from CNN approached me in my finery and asked, "did you ever *used to be* anyone?," I answered, "not yet." But what the hell, I'd just turned seventy and maybe the best was yet to come. If you are reading this book it has. And in the psychic department, Dr. F. was right up there with my mother-in-law.

# CHAPTER 5
## The Rella Cinder Syndrome

Most of the women who wrote to me following the *Times'* column claimed that, like me, they had married in the '50s and early '60s with a set of implied expectations, and found the subsequent realignment of conventions confusing and troubling. For one thing, we usually married as virgins, and couples fled their wedding receptions as soon as the cake was cut, so anxious to rectify that condition. Now brides and grooms dance the night away, the sex thing having been generously taken care of previously.

Also, back then and for centuries before, couples tended to wed at younger ages than now and had babies nine months later. My mother married at eighteen and was barely nineteen when I was born (nine months and two weeks later. Whew!). I was still single at twenty-three and at that advanced age my parents were starting to worry. There was talk of a brochure. So I got married, but when four months later I still wasn't pregnant, they worried some more. My mother tactfully suggested we might explore adoption. My more hard-nosed father indelicately explained that since I'd married a football player he might be sterile on account of "getting kicked in the nuts a lot."

So I prayed and got results, having been directed to seek help from Saint Theresa the Little Flower, my patron saint. You see, Catholics in those days prayed to special saints for special favors. Ours was a very personal religion. We all prayed to Saint Anthony to find lost objects, and Saint Christopher kept our cars from harm's way. My grandmother's spinster sister, Aunt Molly, latched onto the Sacred Heart and everyone in the family received as a Christmas present a magazine called, *Messenger of the Sacred Heart*. When Aunt Molly's godson Joseph was ill, she alerted the Sacred Heart that if anything happened to him she intended to cancel all the subscriptions. Joseph recovered fully. The Sacred Heart knew better than to tangle with Aunt Molly.

But a few years later, when my Uncle Frankie was killed in the war, she turned on Him and switched over to the Infant of Prague who was a unique saint, in that his china statue wore cloth clothing and a gold crown. One Christmas we surprised Aunt Molly with a large and elegantly dressed Infant of Prague and she put it in a place of honor … on top of her Philco TV. Unbeknownst to the family, it took a tumble and the china head cracked off, but Molly fixed it by jamming a pencil down into the statue to perfectly support the head. Who'd know?

Grandma was staying with Molly who insisted they go to church one evening to a novena, but grandma declined because she didn't want to miss Milton Berle. She settled down in front of the TV while a disapproving Molly trotted off to church. Well, a large truck must have rumbled by, and The Infant of Prague began shaking his head from side to side. Grandma grabbed her hat and was off to church in a flash. Such was the power of saints before the Vatican Council deemed the statues irrelevant and Christopher was stripped of his beatification altogether. Superstitiously, we kept him on the dashboard but he was Mr. Christopher now.

The church changed, not for the better, and so did everything else. Once we prayed and patiently waited to be heard, but today instant gratification is expected. Years ago, banks had Christmas Clubs where we saved a few dollars each week to buy holiday gifts. Now we buy first and pay later and later. We know the baby's sex months before it's born and the pictures of the embryo (which I can never decipher) can be developed in seconds. Potatoes can be baked in minutes and soup doesn't have to simmer for hours.

We've adjusted to the practical realities in regard to the potato and the soup, but unfortunately, we tend to carry that over to having less patience with our more complex relationships, which are often scuttled the minute they become thorny. And we suffer the pain of shattered hopes because of our unrealistic expectations.

The wisest woman I know, my Russian friend Galia, is my gold standard and has words of wisdom for almost every occasion, usually gleaned from the Bible or mythology or the classics. But her phrase that consoles me every day is, "You Can't Get Pizza From a Chinese Restaurant." Think about it. Most of the searing disappointments we face are because we've had unrealistic expectations. Of our parents, our siblings, our children, our bosses, our friends. Our spouses. It is an absolute truth that no one can give you what they just don't have. When it comes to relationships, we might call to mind the immortal words of Andrew Jackson at the Battle of New Orleans. "You gotta elevate them sights a little lower."

In our society, unrealistic expectations are richly fueled by popular myths, which we, as parents often loathe to debunk. Take for instance the Cinderella scenario. A great proportion of popular fiction and especially film harkens back to this (think *Pretty Woman, My Fair Lady and Sabrina* -- there are hundreds). Every bride feels like Cinderella, complete with the most expensive dress she'll probably ever wear, and the only limousine she'll probably ever ride in. And looking better than she probably ever looked before. One of my sons tells every groom to take a long look as his bride, she'll never be this thin again. Which testifies to the old adage that, 'women marry hoping their grooms will change and men marry hoping their brides won't change.'

The truth is most modern young women will live the Cinderella scenario in reverse. Rella Cinder. Only a small proportion of them will have dealt with the daily grind of housework and cooking and laundry and child care before marriage. Their days of drudgery will come after the ball. Shattered illusions are inevitable. I remember returning from my honeymoon to our little apartment near Georgetown and there was only one pillow on the king-size bed. My new husband tucked it under his head and said, "goodnight." The honeymoon was over.

Too often, today's bride, however well-educated and sophisticated, buys into the fiction that marriage will solve most of her problems as she goes off with Prince Charming to live happily ever after. In truth, she's embarking on a modern marriage where she'll probably work harder than her mother ever did, because she'll have to juggle a husband and babies and a job. Even without a job, today's children will be high maintenance, requiring constant chauffeuring to parties, classes, play dates, doctors and, often, therapists. And remember she married Prince

Charming ... not Prince Dependable. So her expectations may not be met, and neither will her husband's.

Young women are usually fixated on one day being a bride. They buy *Brides* magazine and scheme and dream about every aspect of their weddings. Have you ever seen a magazine called *Grooms?* Young men buy *Playboy* and *Sports Illustrated's* Swimsuit issue and usually focus on the sexual satisfaction side of marriage. Poor devils. Talk about unrealistic expectations.

Pliny the Younger claimed, "An object in possession seldom retains the charm it had in pursuit." The new husband may think he's married the woman of his dreams, but her family can be more in the nightmare range. And his wife seems to stand behind him all right but it's so she can push. She claims faultless taste while he reveals tasteless faults.

One of my friends had married late in life to a gentlemanly widower who courted her for a year. As they drove off on their honeymoon, he rolled down the car window and gave a loud cough and spit. He did this every five miles or so explaining he had a sinus condition. Not once in the year of dating had he spit. His new wife wondered why he hadn't choked to death. But the score evened later that night when he had to accept, that years of walking the floor at Lord and Taylor's had left his bride with roughly callused and bunioned feet. The result was that when he crept into their marriage bed and snuggled up to her he gently whispered, "you forgot to take your shoes off."

There's a lot of disillusionment. But what did you expect? At least in those bygone days you expected security -- a safety net. He will support me. She will take care of me. That was the implied contract in the halcyon days before pre-nup agreements. Marriage is not the refuge it once was. Today's young women usually have rewarding and interesting jobs. They live independently and they travel and buy good clothes and have sex on their terms and the world's their oyster. But, they have nagging doubts, and eventually want a husband and children and fear that most dreaded label ... old maid.

So they face compromise. In most urban centers young single women are sellers in a buyer's market. There are only a few spots where men outnumber women, like Alaska (where it is said the odds are good but the goods are odd). It's patently unfair. Men don't have biological clocks with stopwatch attachments on their parenting years. Men don't choose between being full-time fathers or working fathers. And more often than not, men still, in these liberated times, expect to be taken care of and women still expect to do that.

Another common disenchantment follows that optimistic phrase, "I'm marrying my best friend." I'm told it does happen but I've never seen it. One of my happily married nieces told me the best advice her mother gave her was not to tell her husband the whole lot. Love and absolute honesty are rarely compatible. Brides don't set out to be deceptive. They want to share *everything* … to tell him the truth. But he just can't handle it. A neighbor with decades of a successful marriage behind her told me that her husband mused that if anything ever happened to her, he'd be losing his best friend. She confided that, much as she loved him, the only way she could see this work in reverse would be if he went down in flames on the same plane as her bridge club.

The thing is, in every close relationship but especially in marriage, one partner can't take bad news and so the other has to organize cover-ups. The trick is to be the one who grabs option one first … early in the partnership take the role of the one who goes to pieces and then your mate has to pick them up. Too often the husband takes that preferred position and the wife spends the rest of her life hiding plumbers' bills and report cards. As much as she loves him and didn't start out to be scheming, survival demands she become manipulative. And eventually she gets really good at it.

My mother's brother Frankie had a rough time in high school and was held back for a fifth year. Unfortunately, he was in a parochial school requiring tuition and when my grandfather was presented with the bill he asked grandma if Frankie shouldn't be graduating. Grandma laced into him, "Glory be to God, didn't he just start a few years ago? When are you going to start paying attention to our children's education?" Grandpa apologized and was so chagrined that he didn't question when, two years later, he paid for a fifth year for his son Johnny.

Some things never change. A 2005 survey by *Money Magazine* found that seventy-one percent of 1,001 women and men with incomes of $50,000 or more admitted keeping money secrets — and, anywhere from thirty to sixty percent of spouses stash money unbeknownst to their partners. This is behavior that transcends gender.

Sometimes it is the wife who is unable to handle crises and then the husband has to take it on the chin. I remember one of my Irish uncles who moaned that he was burdened with hiding every problem from his wife, because at the first hint of trouble, "off goes her head and on goes a windmill." Smart woman!

Implied hysteria can be a winner. A cousin called me one day and said her oldest son had arrived home from college for Christmas wearing an earring. She knew her conservative husband would hit the ceiling and the family's Christmas would be ruined. My advice was, "call his secretary and say you're on your way into his office in the city. He'll have to cancel appointments. It's urgent that you see him immediately. Then when you get there, finding him frantic with worry, you'll blurt out the terrible thing that's happened and how devastated you are. And he'll have no recourse but to say how silly to get so upset over a little thing like an earring. Women!!" Joyeux Noel!

My thirty-something niece told her mother that she wanted to get married, so that when she came home from work at night, she could share everything that happened that day with someone. Her mother replied that, in that case, she should move right back home with her. The thing about most husbands is you can talk to them all right. It's just that they don't listen.

When my children were small (I had my first four in four years), I couldn't wait for my husband to get home so I could converse with an adult. But I soon realized that I'd just as well be talking to the north door of the church. So one night I told him in detail about the gorilla I'd found under the sink, who was finally persuaded to come out and do the Charleston, and my husband said, "that's nice."

# CHAPTER 6
# The Madam was Adam

On the first day of a college psychology course, the professor wrote on the blackboard, "personality is 100% learned," and coming from Catholic schooling I, for the first time ever, openly disagreed with a teacher. I was the oldest of six children and had seen my siblings born with defined personalities. One infant arrived, with clenched fists that are still clenched sixty years later. One, smiling and cooing, has always been congenial. A few years later, there were questionable biological conclusions generated by the Feminist Revolution, noting there is no intrinsic difference between males and females, but females had been conditioned to behave in a subservient manner. Again, I had to disagree.

In her amazing book, *The Female Brain,* Louann Brizendine reports research indicating that all humans begin with brains that look female. Then about the eighth week, testosterone surges through male brains killing cells in some regions (communications) and growing cells in others (sex and aggression). At three months, girls are better at making eye contact and as teens, flushed with estrogen, they have an intense desire to forge connections … to create community and organize their worlds so that they are the center of it.

It's a fascinating study, but the bottom line is men and women are just different. My own sorry situation could not be completely blamed on the Women's Liberation Movement but was, in part, a consequence of the resulting shifting sands of male/female relationships. So I began to speculate on how and why we've come to a point in the evolution of our species, where, in the course of one generation, almost all the

31

gender-based rules have changed. And will continue to change. And wonder, how did those rules and roles originate?

It's understandable that the disparity of the sexes might cause some people to think men and women are from separate planets. But I watch the Sci-Fi network and those creatures would need major overhauling before they could take one of our species out to dinner, never mind mate with them. And those E.T.s are intrinsically cerebral and serene in their demeanor, while our sex act demands more primitive instincts and discombobulating friction. Having dismissed galactic differences, I was led to the sensible conclusion that men and women are more likely dimorphic creatures at different stages of evolution. Which brought me back to my first book.

That book was originally titled, "Occupation Housewife ... Memoir of an Endangered Species," but someone at the publisher's back then decided that both "housewife" and "memoir" had negative connotations, so it was renamed, "Ever Since Adam and Eve." Up to that point I'd never given much thought to this pair. Because unlike some other biblical events, i.e. Christmas and Easter, the Creation had not inspired a shopping opportunity, and the bit with the apple seemed dicey, even to a first grader in Saint Rose of Lima's in Brooklyn.

Whatever the conflict over evolutionary algorithm -- intelligent design vs. evolution -- it's clear some force created each earthly species, and while I prefer to think of that force as God, another might prefer Mother Nature or the Big Bang. For simplicity's sake, let's take my God as the greatest designer ever, said to have created Adam as the first human being ever. Then, when God decided to invent procreation, God created a mate whose body would have to be retrofitted for a sex act. So, obviously God's premiere creation, made in God's image and likeness, was the female with a lithe form, which spreads new light on why men got useless nipples.

My gynecologist tells me that every embryo begins as a female and that a Y chromosome comes along later, and then, unfair but true, from the moment of conception, males are less likely to survive than females. In addition to this inequitable birth advantage, women have a more vigorous immune system than men. So we girls are demonstrably healthier and have greater longevity than guys.

I began writing about the female as the original sex with tongue firmly planted in cheek, but the more I researched the subject, the more I became convinced I was on to something. It just makes sense that when coitus became an issue, God created the male with dangling parts between his legs that were definitely elective ornaments. Which might explain why men are constantly reaching down there to make sure the "attachments" are still affixed. Thus was facilitated a reproductive hook-up after quite minor adjustments to the female. It makes no sense that the first and ONLY human being would be outfitted with sensitive external male genitalia requiring hydraulics yet. Is it any wonder men are so conflicted what with all that commotion going on in their jockey shorts?

I think God wisely decided to give the delicate female a sex partner who would also serve her and their progeny as a protector (hence a larger and stronger specimen). He could slay dragons, do the heavy lifting and fix the carburetor. And adore the female Adam, spending subsequent centuries praising her form in poetry and portraits. What female ever composed sonnets about the male form, or songs about the smell of his hair? No, the male was clearly created to complement the female in every meaning of that word.

Once you get that part right, the apple thing begins to make sense. Would any woman jeopardize a swell home like the Garden of Eden for a bite of forbidden fruit? I personally knew a woman who starved herself to stay a size six to avoid possible ejection from a split ranch in Levittown. Women value their nests. And women are not prone to react to dares, they're too pragmatic. But say, "I dare you" to a man, and there's no holding him back. It was definitely the guy who bit the apple. That clinched the whole Adam and Eve gender thing for me.

Women must be the premiere sex because they are demonstrably higher evolved. They have less body hair and what they have mostly comes out the top of their heads. Unlike the well-known three stages of a man's hair ... unparted, parted and departed. And as their domes grow less hirsute, they can't keep up with the bristles sprouting from their noses and ears and eyebrows. Men are more unrealistically vain than women, or they wouldn't delude themselves, that combing hair over their bald spot fools anyone but themselves. I served on a committee with a middle-aged man who returned from his college reunion disappointed, because "most of my classmates got so fat and bald they didn't recognize me."

The evidence mounts that women are more developed than men. In every species, the female lives longer. Women are able to multi-task and are more detail-oriented. How else can you explain that a man is able to zero in on an asteroid one million light years off, but can't locate the catsup in the refrigerator? He can differentiate between three hundred species of earthworm, but can't recognize his own cousins at the family picnic. He cannot, for the life of him, remember what upset his wife at dinner last night but can recall every stroke he took in a golf game two years ago.

It's because he has more primitive priorities and competition counts for more than feelings. It's the evolution thing. Men are not yet completed. They remain fiercely engaged in areas women are too advanced to take seriously, then celebrate triumphs by pouring Gatorade over each other. They will switch wives and careers because of unrealized expectations but remain fiercely loyal to the Chicago White Sox. If men were not still saddled with the vestiges of primitive phylogeny, would they flock to Pamplona to be chased down narrow streets by five hundred tons of angry pot roast?

Stuck in the macho track, men are more likely to be imprisoned than women. More likely to fly into rages, and a hundred percent more likely to be serial killers. Why? Because men's brains are hard wired for primitive emotions most women have outgrown. And part of their genetic code also leads them to be more obsessed with sex. Please see Chapter 8.

It has always seemed that in the game of life, men were the amateurs and women the professionals. Women are more complex with shorter distances from one emotion to another. While men have been proven to be better detectors of anger and threats, women are more adept at detecting socially relevant expressions communicating happiness, sadness, surprise and disgust.

I was not surprised to learn that there are proven differences between the cognitive skills of men and women. It always amazed me, that when we went out with another couple and the husbands chatted in the front seat and the wives in the back, Jack and I came home with very divergent ideas about our friends. He would say something like, "well, Fred sure has the world by the tail. His business is great and his kids are terrific. I envy that guy." Whereas I reported, "poor Helen. Fred's company is being sold and he'll probably be redundant, their oldest boy is headed for rehab and they're pretty sure young Missy is pregnant." I always contended that I had more meaningful conversations with strangers on supermarket checkout lines than most men have with their closest friends.

One analogy that comes to mind is that, men's lives are express trains, and women's are locals. Having started out as hunters and gatherers, men could have narrowly defined goals and career objectives, and go after them with minimal distractions. Whereas, women's goals were smaller and more immediate ... cook breakfast, dress the kids, pound the laundry on the rocks etc. But women almost always also served as the engine of this train of life, giving it direction and purpose. Keeping it on track. It's historically true that men discovered new territories but women civilized them.

Men and women are equal, but women are simply more evolved. Just think about violence. That is a male trait, as evidenced by the number of women in jails as compared to men -- and there are credible theories that most incarcerated women are there because they were aiding or abetting their criminal men folk. Or had murdered them. I even heard a rational explanation of something called a "Sir Tax" by an economist who claimed that men should pay higher income taxes than women, because they place the greater burden on the costly criminal justice system. Pointing out that women pay lower car insurance rates than men because they cause fewer accidents, and with this paradigm, it only follows that they pay less income taxes.

The poor less-evolved devils not only have this aggressive streak to control, but they face hurdles in other less profound areas. For instance, men are greater gossips and better storytellers than women and would enjoy the soap opera and family saga type stories on television. But they can't. Because men watching TV are incapable of keeping track of more than two people at a time unless they have numbers on their backs. I have an idea for a soap opera aimed at men where not only would the actors wear numbers, but little trailers would appear every time a new character came on the scene; "Larry who used to be married to Betty before he had the sex change operation that turned her into

Nancy who is now engaged to Fred." The show would be marketed as, "Closed-captioned for the gender impaired."

# CHAPTER 7
# Men and Why Women Love Them

Evolution notwithstanding, it seems obvious to me that historically and psychologically, men and women need and complement each other. In all of the letters I received from women disappointed by the men in their lives, not one disparaged all men, or regretted having been married. Most had loved their husbands, many still did, and were still trying to figure out what happened.

If I sounded like I was male-bashing with my 'Madam Was Adam' theory, well I wasn't. I never could do that anyway because I have the gangs of four -- four brothers, four sons and four grandsons. And, because like most women of my era, my life was defined by the men in it. I went right from being John Martin's daughter, to being Jack Hekker's wife, to Jackie Hekker's mother.

When I wrote that piece for the *Times'* Op-Ed page in '77 it required a two-line bio, and I identified myself with, "*Terry Martin Hekker has been married for 22 years. Her husband Jack Hekker is a lawyer who has been a South Nyack Village Judge for 14 years.*" It was never about me. And it was ok. That was the way it was for women then, because we were supporting players to the men who were our protectors and providers.

As a protector and provider, my father overshot the runway and he imbedded in us two phrases. Never underestimate the utility of virtue and never resist a generous impulse. He was an extraordinary man and the driving force in my life -- an astonishing character. He managed the Bear Mountain Inn, a few miles south of West Point in New York's Hudson Valley, which served as a training camp for athletes (the Brooklyn Dodgers, the Giants football team, the Knicks, the Golden

Glovers, etc.). Leo Durocher played poker with my grandmother (she took a few bucks from him) and we knew Frank Gifford before Kathie Lee was born. Living there was a fabulous and unique experience.

I was raised in an atmosphere reeking of testosterone, which gave me a powerful appreciation for all things male. I have come to believe that, having created the female first, God had time to reflect on what features She might have overlooked with the first human. And, to compensate for the male being the "sex-driven second sex," God gave men their magnificent and heroic traits. Their gallantry. Their physical strength and their own unique beauty and grace, and their imagination and artistic and intellectual gifts.

Also, in creating the second sex and procreation, God knew there would be trouble ahead. While the female was given almost instant maturity, coping mechanisms and a divine ability to nurture children, she often lacked the spirit of innovation and imagination that would be required down the line. And, consumed with caring for children, she rarely had been given the fierce single-minded tenacity required to pursue great dreams.

If there had been a fine female artist in Rome in 1481 and Pope Sixtus IV had proposed that she paint the story of creation, he might have struck a deal. But when he said he wanted it painted on a chapel ceiling sixty-feet high, forget it. The response would probably be along the lines of, "you've got to be kidding" (shouted in Italian with gestures).

Just imagine a group of women lounging around the Spanish Court in 1492 and one of them saying, "You know girls, I've had a feeling the earth may actually be round not flat. How about we get us some boats and head west and see if we fall off." Even the Queen wouldn't have bought that. It took a man to do it and a man to talk the Queen into paying for it. Which is one of the other great gifts God gave men -- the ability to talk a woman into almost anything.

An aside on this subject, the advice I give my teenage granddaughters is to watch Judge Judy. On any given day, many of the problems she tries to solve concern a young woman who has been victimized by a man who borrowed money or moved in with her and/or emptied her bank account. Often pointing out how unappealing and lacking in charm these predators are, Judge Judy asks these girls "what were you thinking?", and, "please tell me you've learned a lesson." I love Judge Judy.

Returning to men and their creativity and curiosity, in 1613, a female Galileo, however scientifically gifted, would probably have concluded that no one really cared that the path of a projectile is a parabola and would have called it a day. A female Beethoven in 1800 would not have said to her family, "Okay guys, you're on your own for dinner for the next month while I write my Ninth Symphony." She wouldn't have gotten past Number One.

And think of Thomas Edison and what he gave us -- almost every laborsaving device we cherish today resulted from his ability to focus on inventing while Mrs. E. kept the home fires burning. I heard from someone who'd researched Edison that he had a passion for expensive cigars and kept a box of them on his desk. When he noticed they were disappearing at an alarming rate he bought a box of "joke cigars" -- disgustingly fashioned out of old rope and kerosene -- and put them out on his desk to discourage the pilfering. Then later realized, that because his mind was so concentrated elsewhere, he'd smoked every one of them himself.

The examples are endless. With some notable exceptions, the great artists have been men, also most of them were great inventors, explorers, composers, philosophers and writers. And while we could say that historically women were too repressed to pursue grand creativity, I have not noticed any surge of female imagination in the last fifty years when women have been encouraged to enter all the formerly male arenas. They've successfully done so in professions you might think were exclusive to men because of the required physical strength, becoming firefighters and policewomen and soldiers.

Women have proved excellent administrators, politicians, prime ministers, secretaries of state, judges. But again with a few exceptions, they have not written the great modern music or painted masterpieces. Or scooped up Pulitzer and Nobel Prizes. Although demonstrably more nonviolent by nature than males, in the entire twentieth century only six women won the Peace Prize and only one -- Mother Teresa -- was the sole winner, not half of a duo.

However, it must be noted that women often know instinctively what men take years of research to discover. Decades before Thomas

Watson identified DNA's presence in saliva, my grandmother knew when a baby was "the spitting image" of a relative. With some regularity, scientists call press conferences to announce breakthroughs in healthcare having determined methodically that chicken soup does have therapeutic properties and wet feet *can* cause you to catch a cold. In February 2004, Pfizer Pharmaceuticals announced it was abandoning its million-dollar effort to prove its drug, Viagra, would be beneficial to females. Their researchers had discovered that men and women have "fundamentally different relationships between arousal and desire." Another case where grandma wouldn't have paid a nickel for that news.

Despite good instincts and uncanny intuition, women are often too grounded and practical to pursue the bravura dreams that men follow. Too distracted by living, which probably gives them happier lives than men so often obsessed with unattainable goals. So if men can't find the catsup in the refrigerator, they can find new worlds. If they can't find their car keys, they can find a cure for polio. They should be celebrated for their God-given gifts that have benefited and enriched our world for all these centuries. In ways no female could have done.

And men have an overriding compulsion to be our heroes -- our protectors and saviors. They make great fathers, providing security and the drive and energy their children need to grow. While mothers have a tendency to say, "Junior, that's a great picture you drew," the father adds, "but you'll never make a living drawing headless snakes." Mothers and fathers both nurture but in different and complementary ways. Teaching the competitive component of life is usually the male job, although he sometimes over shoots the runway, if my grandson's midget hockey team is any example. That pesky testosterone again.

Men also complement women in their coping mechanisms being more adept at picking up signals of anger and threat than women. According to *Psychology Today* (September-October 2000), in extreme situations males tend to choose between *fight and flight*, where females in most species lean to *tend and befriend*. The adaptive value of fighting or fleeing is lower for females who often have dependent young and are not as fleet of foot. So females in many species form tight, stable alliances seeking out friends for support in times of stress. Biologically, if men are the natural warriors, women are the natural peacemakers. If males are more adversarial, females are more consensus builders. And a family, human or animal, benefits from the balance of both traits.

As the mother of three men who are terrific fathers, it annoys me that so many TV commercials portray daddy as the dunce whose wife and children always outsmart him. Most fathers I know are concerned protectors who unselfishly provide for their families. They make terrific partners for us girls, although too often distracted by their consuming need for sex and other built-in obsessions that are the remnants of their early roles as hunters. Which explains why some men are so fascinated with hunting that they'll spend hundreds of dollars to outfit a trip into the marshes to shoot a duck, when for a few bucks, they could buy one oven-ready in the market down the block. And that conjures up men and golf … the hunter redux.

I must admit to a personal prejudice against golf. It began about fifteen years ago when I still thought I had a good marriage. My husband suffered an aortic aneurysm and was saved by a surgeon who had to slice him from chest to thigh. On his first post-operative visit, the doctor asked to speak to both of us because he had to explain that the surgery might result in certain restrictions. It could cause impotence. Jack heaved a great sigh of relief and said, "oh thank God. I was afraid you were going to tell me I can't play golf any more." As I said, there was handwriting on the wall.

I figured out that golf really isn't a sport at all but a kind of return to the caveman trip for many men. Think about the terminology. Men play tennis. They play ball. But they *shoot* a round of golf. They're out in the fields, carrying sticks with metal bottoms (the reverse of rifles that are sticks with metal at the top). They stealthily hunt a small ball. In fact, the great Irish philosopher Hal Roach observed, "golf is played by men with small balls." They demand absolute silence as they concentrate on whacking one. Golf's great defender P.G. Wodehouse wrote, "the talking golfer is undeniably the most pronounced pest of our complex civilization." Once the game is completed, however, there is endless chatter about that round. Wodehouse attests that, "women have to learn to bear (golfing) anecdotes from the men they love. It's the curse of Eve." There's that evolution thing again.

There are women who enjoy golf and God bless them. But most golf clubs are male bastions with governing boards as gender balanced as the College of Cardinals. With rules those Cardinals would approve because golf is more than a pastime or a sport. It is an ersatz religion inspiring absolute devotion. A golf course is maintained and venerated like an outdoor cathedral. Golfers are zealots whose detractors are Philistines. The patron is Saint Andrew and its vestments, liturgy and rubrics (the niblick, the bogey, the birdy, the mulligan) are sacred and prescribed. Golf tournaments on television are reported in whispers, like a Pope's funeral.

Golf does not demand vestments, but it does require a mode of dress unacceptable in any other arena. The average male golfer wears clothes that would make Corporal Klinger wince. And as bizarre as some of their wildly colored outfits might appear, they are essentially standardized -- they all seem to dress alike. Compared to the average club golfer, the Rockettes look like rugged individualists. And those hats. Golf hats can make the most attractive man look like a dork. Think Cary Grant in a golf hat. While guys playing manly sports can be wildly attractive to women, generally speaking, the most sex-starved female could not be turned on by a fully outfitted golfer.

I can't let the subject of golf end without this profound comment from my sainted Aunt Adelaide who played her first round of golf on a senior citizen's outing when she was eighty. Her commentary encapsulated all my thoughts on the subject. An Irish born devout Catholic she proclaimed, "golf was nice. It reminded me a lot of the Stations of the Cross. But I'd just rather do the Stations of the Cross."

# CHAPTER 8
## Sex and the Possible

Further following up on my Madam was Adam theory, if indeed men were created primarily for procreation of the species, then they shouldn't be castigated for their abiding interest in sex. While attitudes toward sex may have changed dramatically, once again the basic dynamic remains unchanged and often unappreciated. I admit this is a subject about which my personal experience is limited. Very limited.

I married at twenty-three and was a virgin until my wedding night. Then forty years later when I was single again the subject was moot. There was a soft market for sixty-three year old grandmothers in support hose and frankly there was no point in looking for Mr. Right. He'd just divorced me. And then there was the philosophical issue … what would be gained by trying sex with someone new? Having known only the one man in the biblical sense, I couldn't gauge whether my husband was a great or lousy lover. And I grasped that there was no percentage in finding out. If a new relationship showed him to be, comparatively, a rotten lover, then I'd be depressed that I'd missed so much for so long. If it proved him to be a terrific lover, I'd be even more disheartened that I'd never have a go at it again. Either way I lost.

But there's one thing I do know about sex. It is more imperative to men than the majority of females understand. On top of that, many men have a tough time with monogamy, even though it is practiced successfully by the chinstrap penguin, the long eared owl, the mantis shrimp and the black vulture. Monogamy is rare, because it can thrive only in the styles of life where male and female interests are closely aligned, which doesn't always fit with our modern social order. Also, there is increasing evidence that the sexual genetic differences between men and women are greater than previously recognized.

Growing up in the 1940s and '50s, pre-marital sex was not an issue. It was simply out of the question. But as our sons headed off to college in the late '70s, in the age of AIDS, their father had to confront certain realities. Having no experience in this eventuality, he groped about and finally decided to explain condoms to our hockey-playing sons as, "goalies in the mating game."

My advice to my daughter was pretty much the same as my mother gave me. She had asked if I knew where babies came from, and when I answered yes, she said, "good. Don't have any."

For most women sex is essential and vital. Given the times I grew up in, I can only imagine it's fun when they're single and certainly it's icing on the wedding cake. For men, it is a consuming compulsion because they were fashioned by their maker with their raison d'etre being sex and reproduction. It is undoubtedly the reason why men's sexual satisfaction, ejaculation, has everything to do with procreation, while women's orgasms have absolutely nothing to do with making babies.

Teenage boys are consumed with girls' bodies. They share X-rated magazines and films. I don't ever remember a young girl aching to see pictures of nude men, or looking through a peephole into the men's locker room. That is why it's so ludicrous that men think there is such a thing as penis envy. Although they come in handy at a picnic, women not only don't want them, they're not anxious to even catch sight of them until the time is exactly right.

The daughter of a friend, trying to decide whether to marry a young man who'd proposed, asked her eight-nine year old Italian grandmother how to tell if you're in love. Her grandmother replied, "it's easy. If he put his *thing* near you and you didn't mind, you'd have to be in love. It's so ugly. Like an old chicken neck." My grandmother, being teased about peeking at a nude streaker (remember them?) announced, "I'd rather see a ghost." So much for the Full Monty. And my own reaction is that, having four younger brothers and four sons, naked men were never an erotic image. When I saw a naked man, my first thought was LAUNDRY. Because I knew somewhere he'd left me a disgusting pile of it.

But beauty lies you know where. With the possible exception of circus contortionists, most women have never even seen their genitals, but men can be consumed with the appearance of theirs. Especially the size. Doesn't it explain a lot that among themselves men often refer to their genitals as their "jewels?" They even name their penises. Like "Willie the One-Eyed Worm." Or, "Mr. Happy." When I first heard the phrase "joy stick" it didn't occur to me it was part of a video game. It seemed such a perfect name for a penis that provides the owner with delight from infancy to the grave.

Any mother of a son knows the glee with which a baby boy first discovers his penis, and that delight only increases with age. I overheard a friend of my son's complaining that his lawyer wife is so paranoid about their nanny possibly abusing their baby, that she planted hidden TV cameras all over the house. The husband's gripe with this -- he couldn't find a safe place to masturbate. The guys all nodded with empathy.

Our media has an obsession with sex. Pornography is a huge industry and even mainstream magazine racks are full of it. Television is consumed by it and I don't just mean the more raunchy cable programs. I am a big fan of *Everybody Loves Raymond,* a good family show, and Ray is always begging for sex, which I find amusing and real. But can you imagine Beaver's parents or Ozzie and Harriet even mentioning their sex life? From Ozzie Nelson to Ozzie Osborne, we've come a long way.

I would never trivialize the sex act. It is wondrous and terrific and quite indescribable. But as exciting as it is, it's hardly the be-all and end-all. Orgasm is a grand experience, but it can be self-induced and in this form, can be both satisfying and simplified. As Woody Allen says, it's sex with someone you really care about. And you don't have to look your best. (It continues to mystify me that, what the rest of the world calls "self-gratification," the Catholic Church refers to as "self-abuse.") But while Mother Nature made orgasm self-achievable, she fixed it so we get no pleasure from holding our own hand or hugging ourselves. We can't even tickle ourselves, never mind pat our own backs. That's where affection and love come in.

Why then all the sex manuals? I've read many of them (strictly for research purposes) and find them as uniformly erotic as the directions that came with my Home Depot storage racks. "Insert part one in slot in part six." As they get more graphic, there are high marks awarded to technique. But since the primary sexual organ is the brain, physical performance that's rated like an Olympic event (eight points for style, six points for presentation and seven points for a clean dismount) seems ludicrous.

I've known young women who claim they have sex with a man so he'll talk to them. Become involved with them. How's that for an unrealistic expectation? What men want out of the sex act is almost the exact opposite of what women want, unless there is a real connect between them. A young man explained to me that even in this age of sexual permissiveness, when a guy can almost always pick up a girl in a bar who'll go to bed with him, he still turns to prostitutes. He said, "we don't pay them for the sex, we pay them to go away afterwards."

Decades ago when there was a TV expose on the *real* best little whorehouse in Texas, a townswoman told the interviewer that she was happy her husband had someplace to go and take care of his needs. Face it, many men have preexisting sexual urges that their loving wives cannot satisfy. Itches their wives cannot scratch.

And truth be told, many women don't have sex as their primary concern. One of my friends confessed that when she was first married, she'd break out with cold sores from excitement when her husband was about to make love to her. And now she gets them in the furniture department at Bloomingdales. Things change!

A few years back, our nation went through a constitutional crisis when it became known that a high-level elected official received oral sex from a young woman in his oddly shaped office. Turned out the office wasn't the only thing oddly shaped, but never mind, there was great consternation in our nation. Two of my male doctor friends were shocked that none of their married female patients seemed to have a problem with this. I explained that as a marital duty, oral sex can be right up there with cleaning the oven. There's a reason it's referred to as a "job." I'm sure some women enjoy it -- truly enjoy giving pleasure to their husbands. But I have never met a wife who looked forward to doing it. And in my AFGO group, every one of us would have been thrilled if pursuing that form of satisfaction was the worst sin our husbands had committed.

46

Women of my generation never spoke about oral sex or any other kind for that matter. But I've heard younger women say things like, "today's my husband's birthday and you know what that means. You know what he wants. Oh God!" An Irish woman explained that over there it's called, "playing the dreaded skin flute." There are many terms of art for this sex act, but in my day none of them were mentioned. Then at the height of the 'Monica discourse', when a group of my women friends finally alluded to the fact that they hadn't ever personally enjoyed giving oral sex, one of the shyest women in the room blurted out, "and I really hate the view."

But oral sex was not the only thing we didn't talk about. In Irish homes, the sex act itself was rarely even alluded to. When a cousin became pregnant before her wedding day, I heard it said that her boyfriend had "interfered" with her. And once my grandmother commented on a lacy nightgown unwrapped at a bridal shower, "that doesn't look like it'll take much tuggin and haulin." It happened to be my nightgown and she was right.

If they used the word "vagina" I never heard it. I recall that one of my mother's cousins was plagued with yeast infections and that she had trouble again with her "homa-hoska doodle." I swear to you, that was the term of reference. And if that sounds bizarre, consider the six-syllable Irish folklore term for the penis -- domfostimacatur. You couldn't make that up.

As I wrote this chapter, I realized it's the first time I ever typed the word "penis." My brothers had willys. My sons had jiggys. Which was why I could relate, when my old friend Patsy told me about training to be a nurse in the fifties in a Catholic hospital, where a nun lectured the students about how to give a man a sponge bath. She told the girls, "start at the top of his head and wash as far down as possible. Then begin at his feet and wash as far up as possible. DON'T TOUCH POSSIBLE."

# CHAPTER 9
## Divorcees vs. Widows: The Dichotomy

There were days when I would have killed – literally -- to be a widow. And many of the women who contacted me after *The Times'* column shared that sentiment. But in the realm of available life choices, most married women do not get to select whether they'll end their lives as divorcees or widows. However, statistically, most will end up alone, and whether her husband left her for the hereafter or the whoever, an ex-wife will be forced to re-invent her life. But that will be in many ways easier, if more sorrowful for the widows than the divorcees.

Girls in my generation, especially Catholic girls, never expected to be divorced but we did rather expect to live our last years alone as widows. And some women looked forward to that. For the past decade I have taken to ask my most happily married women friends, "if anything, God forbid, happened to your husband, would * you think about remarrying?" The * marks the point at which they shouted, "*NO!*" It's like my grandmother used to say about having babies, "I wouldn't take a million dollars for the ones I have and I wouldn't give a nickel for another one."

The myth of man-hungry widows stalking any fellow still breathing is just that … at least in my world. While in the Ladies Room of a Manhattan theater, I ran into a recently widowed old friend who seemed to be doing all right, and I asked her, "would you ever think of getting married again?" The occupants of six stalls and eight women still on line all shouted, *"NO!"*

While both widows and divorcees benefit from doubling of their closet space and access to the bottom shelf in the medicine cabinet, there are defining differences. For instance, while most married women complain that their husbands are occasionally thoughtless, selfish and immature, most widows were married to saints. Once he's six feet under, virtues are celebrated that never surfaced previously.

I had an aunt and uncle who fought constantly and vociferously, but at his wake, as she stood tearfully by his casket, she remarked to every passing mourner, "and wasn't he a martyr to piles." I never figured out whether she was attempting to gain him sympathy or humiliate him -- their relationship was hardly cordial. The truth was every time I drove them anywhere, I made them sit one in the front seat and one in the back, and even then they swatted at each other. But on the way home from the cemetery after my uncle's funeral, my aunt said, I swear, "wasn't Packy a grand man! And never a cross word between us." I thought she was indulging in a little black humor. She wasn't. She'd become a widow.

There is this phenomenon called, "Sanctification of the Deceased Spouse." Wives whose meals verged on the poisonous are transformed by death into gourmet cooks. Husbands who were all thumbs are portrayed as gifted handymen. Widows remember husbands as sensitive and protective, while the assessment that leaps to your mind is boorish and self-centered. Widowers were married to classic beauties -- depending on the coloring, their late wives were dead ringers for Grace Kelly or Elizabeth Taylor -- although photographs indicate marked resemblance to Dame Edna. As a housekeeper, he thinks Hazel and you think Mrs. Danvers. Conversely, after divorce the wife never understood him and was an appalling homemaker, and the ex-husband, hereafter referred to as "the bum," is vilified with no statute of limitations.

If it's true that most widows were married to Sir Lancelot, most divorcees were married to the back end of his horse. Speaking about their wedding days, they'll refer to the groom as "that jerk." Decades of a reasonably happy marriage are forgotten after he trots off with another woman (or man). This is most unfortunate because it only fuels resentments when a woman says -- and believes -- "I wasted thirty years on that bum." First off, he wasn't a bum when you married him, and if you raised children together, that wasn't a waste of time. Resentment is counterproductive. There's an Irish saying, "Resentment is like swallowing poison and expecting the other fella to die."

I would have been a terrific widow. To be honest, I sort of planned on it. As the oldest member of two big families, I have arranged more than a few funerals and have, in desperate times, considered advertising myself as a *Funeral Planner*. After all there's a market for Wedding Planners and the lead time for a wedding is about a year; while the lead time for a funeral is, tops, two days ... all the more reason to contact a pro like me. And, coming from a big Irish family, I have black outfits for every season plus a strong belief in the hereafter, so death is not an end but a beginning, which tends to make me a tad more tranquil.

With widow's weeds at the ready, divorce was just not in my plan and I hate the distrustful way it makes me feel. To quote Jean Kerr, "being divorced is like being hit by a Mack truck. If you live through it, you start looking very carefully to the right and to the left."

Several of my friends are now widowed, and the agony of losing someone you love who loves you back is horrific. I would never trivialize the pain that accompanies the death of a loved one. But widows have some advantages. For starters, a widow gets the bad news from a sympathetic doctor or clergyman. A divorcee learns her fate from a seedy process server.

A dead husband conforms to the ancient canon, "you can't take it with you." So he routinely leaves behind his earthly belongings and his family and friends. But the divorcee's husband can (and does) take it with him. His money, his credit cards, his relatives and some of hers. Oh, and friends, their family doctor, etc. And if that isn't enough hurt, no matter what the circumstances of her divorce, there are people close to her who have always relied on her husband to do their tax returns, fix their cars or whatever, and they desert her too.

A widow inherits her husband's estate, his social security and his pension. Their home. A dumped wife is, statistically, plunged into poverty. A widow is the object of sympathy and respect whether or not she had a good marriage. A divorcee is suspect no matter how abused she was or how unfairly she was victimized or what caused the break up. She still has to deal with, "there are two sides to every story" (trust me, not always). And unless their friends are clairvoyant or he decides to do that Marley's Ghost bit, a dead husband does not have the opportunity to badmouth his widow. Divorced wives do not benefit from that shield. The operative phrase is, "adding insult to injury."

Whether her marriage was happy or unhappy, a widow is never judged, and becomes an icon in her husband's family. As their last link with a beloved brother or son, she is treated with affection and respect. And she never again has to help with the dishes at family parties. A woman who's been divorced is usually ostracized by her husband's family. Excluded from their lives. No matter how faithful a daughter-in-law she's been, how many holiday turkeys she's cooked, or how attached she's become to those nieces and nephews, she's OUT and her replacement is IN. There was a case in the news a while back where a widow enjoyed the unqualified support of her in-laws even though she'd killed their son (accidentally running over him several times). She wouldn't have that support if he'd divorced her.

On the plus side for divorce, if your husband left he probably hadn't been a lot of laughs lately anyway. And an abusive husband who leaves provides temporary relief. Particularly if his first and prime mistresses have been the exotic types ... Bacardi and Stolichnaya. The divorcee mourns in a different way than her widowed friend, but they both have to seriously reinvent their lives when, after decades as half of a couple, they become first person singular. And the coping mechanisms they've both been forced to adopt are incredibly similar.

Having spent all of my adulthood as half of a pair, I realized that my social life, if I was to have one, demanded rethinking and astute planning. When you have a partner, it's easy to be spontaneous -- let's go to a movie or for a ride in the country or to that new restaurant. So I learned to plan ahead and call someone early in the week to arrange a movie date for the weekend. I found friends with similar tastes and together we bought subscriptions to theater and lecture series ... the cheaper ones.

Living so close to New York City was a huge help; there were all kinds of opportunities for outings. Bookstores offered the chance to meet authors, and museums offered inspiration and enlightenment. And when I realized I was getting bogged down with self-pity, I signed on as a volunteer with agencies that served the mentally challenged and started delivering Meals on Wheels, forcing me to count my abundant blessings.

I also found being single gave me time to forge closer friendships with several extraordinary women who enriched and inspired me.

Women I didn't have the opportunity to know as well while I was married. I reconnected with friends from the past as I acquired new ones, and it was these astonishing women who made all the difference in my resurgence.

The little everyday adjustments were puzzling. On the plus side, I never had to buy Irish Spring soap or salted butter again. But sleep came fitfully, until I began taking my husband's side of the king-size bed so I wasn't reaching over for him. I finally bought a new, smaller bed when I found myself sleeping on the living room couch so I wouldn't feel so alone. That had worked for me until I suspected I was developing an unhealthy relationship with my sofa, as I found myself pressing my spine against its back, inquiring, "so how was your day?"

I learned to turn down any invitation that had the word "dance" in it. Nothing makes you feel sadder than sitting alone at a table while all the couples twirl off. It gets worse when a woman friend shoves her husband toward you whispering, "be nice, ask her." You've become a charity case. A geriatric wallflower. Bringing to mind that great line from *The Man Who Came To Dinner*, "Am I to be spared *nothing?*"

Both widows and divorcees share the disenchantment when their relationships with their married friends change. Widows often experience being invited by old friends for the first few months after they are alone but it usually dwindles off. Divorcees don't even get those few months. At least I didn't. Two couples my husband and I were close enough to vacation with, had never called me again. But unexpectedly, friends from years back came to my rescue. The terrific guy whose date I was on the night I met my husband -- who I abandoned at the Statler Hotel forty-two years ago -- became my real Knight in Shining Armor, offering me consolation, companionship and even financial help.

Widows often say that after a few months they expect their husbands to come back from the dead. It's an acknowledged phenomenon. And they undeniably have better odds on having a spouse return than a divorcee. Well-meaning friends tell you, "Just wait. He'll come crawling back." He doesn't even look back. Especially older men who leave older wives for younger women, twenty-first century foxes, and one last chance to recapture youth. They've left what they see as a marriage running on empty for a high-octane relationship. They're not about to resume cruise control even when that new road taken proves bumpier than projected.

The widow who can envision her spouse plucking a harp in heaven has it all over a divorcee, who has to face her ex clucking over his chippie at family events. It's a true imbroglio. She is flustered. The happy couple gets defensive, then lovey-dovey. And everyone in the room begins to squirm. Especially their children. It's excruciating.

And, let's be honest. Not every widow is consumed with grief. It was a shock to me the first time I tried to comfort a new widow who hastily indicated she was relieved to see the back of him. Then there's that line from Oscar Wilde's *The Importance Of Being Earnest*, where Lady Bracknell says, "I ... (called) on dear Lady Harbury. I hadn't been there since her poor husband's death. I never saw a woman so altered; she looks quite twenty years younger."

Years ago I met a woman who complained about the rotten month she'd had. Her grouchy husband, a former smoker, had been hospitalized because he could barely breathe. And she'd just spend weeks trekking to the hospital, but her two grown children always went with her. I remarked how thoughtful they were -- hospital visiting can be draining -- and she shot back, "oh, they knew if I was ever alone with that bastard I'd kick the plug out of his respirator." Ever since then I've looked suspiciously at anyone whose cranky spouse died unexpectedly.

Do-it-yourself widowhood is a phenomenon I haven't pursued but not for want of clues. I've heard about more than one abusive husband who died in his sleep of an unanticipated heart attack. Once a neighbor I barely knew confided that her husband, dying at home of terminal cancer, needed constant care and when he had any strength to help himself, he picked up the phone to call his girlfriend. So she decided to speed him on his way and mashed up every pill he had into applesauce, fed it to him and went to bed in another bedroom. When she went to him the next morning with high hopes, a death rattle at least, he was sitting up whistling. She admitted it was awfully disappointing, but on the bright side she thought she might have found the cure for cancer.

So, not every woman is devastated by losing her husband, and there can even be an upside to a divorce that was probably preceded by months of tension. My friend Elaine called me almost every night concerned about my health that had been faltering as my marriage lost altitude. One night, weeks after my husband left, I was able to report that I'd had my annual physical and my blood pressure had come down, my anemia was under control, and both the colitis and the shingles had disappeared. Elaine put it all in perspective. "You belong in the f**king *New England Medical Journal*. Four major illnesses cured by a process server."

# CHAPTER 10
## Divorce: Hell in the Hallway

I had been blessed with a privileged life. Although born into a row house in Brooklyn, by the time I was in high school, my father was successful and wealthy. At his hotel, the Bear Mountain Inn, we lived like royalty with cooks and maids to take care of us. Some of the most intriguing persons in the world visited. My mother kept an autograph book that was signed by dozens of celebrities including three United States Presidents.

In the spring of 1944, our family had to move out of our private cottage behind the Inn because it had been rented to Madame Chiang Kai-shek, China's First Lady. President Roosevelt put his personal car at her disposal for that month, but since she rarely used it, the Secret Service Agents, out of sheer boredom, drove me and my brothers to school most mornings. Imagine, the Presidential limousine delivering three kids with their paper-bagged lunches to Sacred Heart School in Highland Falls. We were the cat's meow!

When the war ended and the Dodgers could go back to Florida for '46 spring training, our family joined them, and I have a picture of my friend Ann and myself with our fathers sitting in wooden bleachers watching a Negro baseball game. Ann's mother, Dearie Mulvey, was a part-owner of the Brooklyn Dodgers and they were checking out a player called Jackie Robinson who made history when he joined The Dodgers. Ann later married Ralph Branca who carved his own niche in baseball history.

At spring training in '49, my father had to go back north on business, but left my mother with his big rented Cadillac. At one of the exhibition games in Palm Beach, the Dodger manager Chuck Dressen asked mother if she would give Jackie Robinson and Roy Campanella a lift back to Vero Beach, because the team would be eating supper on the road and the restaurants would not serve Negroes. She and I picked them up at the players' entrance and were heckled unmercifully with the most ugly racial slurs ... two white women inviting two black men into their car. And although I considered my mother elderly at the time, she was in fact only 36 ... nineteen years older than I.

Jackie and Roy were embarrassed for us, and anxious, as a couple of men had banged on the car windows. And, we were mortified for them but that was not something new. Once, we'd been sitting together with Rachel Robinson and her children at a game, when someone threw a black cat on the field and shouted at Jackie, "here's your brother n-----." Jackie had heroic nobility and was always the gentleman, and I often wonder if the Afro-American players of today fully realize what he went through to open doors for them.

Vince Lombardi and his wife Marie used to come to the Inn when he was coaching at West Point, as Marie and my mother were old friends. When he was offered the job as assistant coach with our New York Giants, my father advised Vince that the money might be better, but there was really no place for a guy like him in professional football. He never lived that one down. When Vince moved to Green Bay and won the first Super Bowl, we teased the old man that his advice had been right up there with the guys who told Wilbur and Orville that contraption would never get off the ground.

The Chinese have a saying, "May You Lead An Interesting Life." I thought it was a blessing but have been told the Oriental mind sees it as a curse. In any event, I had a most interesting and even charmed life and am grateful for it. I'm telling these stories not to brag, but to put in context the place I came from, and the depths to which I sank after my husband left me. After a lifetime of financial security, suddenly, overnight, I could not pay my bills. I lost my medical insurance, my credit cards were cancelled and a joint savings account was cleaned out.

I felt like I was in some kind of twilight zone ... walking through a bad dream from which I couldn't seem to wake up. My 'this-can't-be-happening-to-me' feeling wasn't denial but the consequence of the place I came from -- as a Catholic woman married in the mid-fifties. I never expected to be ditched by my husband. It was unthinkable in my "forever after" marriage. I was incredibly naïve and obtuse. The signs were all there. I refused to read them. The best analogy is that if you can't spot the pigeon in a poker game, you're probably it.

Like the hundreds of women who contacted me, my first reaction was an overwhelming feeling of betrayal. Not something I had much experience with until then. But I do now, because you can only be betrayed by someone you trusted (like Judas or Brutus or Linda Tripp). It is one of the most agonizing and hurtful things to face, and being divorced by someone you've given your heart to is the ultimate betrayal. And it gets worse because being rejected by your spouse is only the first in a series of painful betrayals as you find yourself forsaken by people you thought were *your* friends or people you *knew* were your relatives.

When my husband divorced me, I had to face disloyalty, which often came from the most unlikely places. Single women friends exposed their schadenfreude by transmitting an unmistakable, "now you know how I feel" attitude. A childhood friend in whom I had confided my most unmerited and agonizing humiliations shocked me months later, when he cheerily told me, "I played golf with your ex yesterday." I felt like I'd been socked in the stomach. I guarantee that if he'd seen my husband kick a dog he would never have spoken to him again.

This sort of thing was honestly the most agonizing part of the process. That's where the Chinese/pizza line became consoling. Betrayal is not an exact science and some people don't comprehend loyalty -- which is perhaps today's most underrated virtue. You come to understand that ultimately their lives are more diminished by that deficit than yours will ever be. But God does it hurt.

Divorce reflects the deepest disappointment among human relationships. Sophocles said, "the greatest griefs are those we cause ourselves." In the realm of discretionary wounds, divorce is one of the most painful. Like the women who shared their stories with me after the *Times'* piece, nothing had prepared me for this trip to hell and, thankfully, back again. There were no short cuts, no tricks and no anesthetics to ease the agony. Al-Anon has a dizzying assortment of catch phrases plastered around their meeting rooms, and as corny as they look at first glance, they prove life preservers down the line. One of my favorites is, "When One Door Closes Another One Opens, But

It's Hell In The Hallway." That hallway is the perfect metaphor for divorce.

Al-Anon also teaches that we cannot hinge our happiness on getting someone else to change. The only person you can change is yourself and even that can be a daunting job. For me the toughest part was dismissing self-defeating thoughts like self-pity and resentment. Almost every day since my divorce something has surfaced where I have to stop and tell myself, "Let it go." The good news of my divorce was that my children were grown so I had no "dependents," but the bad news was I became dependent on my children for support in all its permutations. Divorce is dramatically easier for childless young couples because once the assets are divided they never have to see each other again. I think of these as small "d" divorces. It's the big "D" divorces that break up a family that are so disruptive.

To my mind, a big "D" divorce is like amputation -- to be considered only as an absolutely last resort when every other option had been explored. Because married couples who share a family can't burn their bridges, their children are on them. The pain to children is almost unbearable whatever their ages; parents' divorce is the seminal event in a child's life. These children have their most basic security torn asunder. Their hurt and distrust takes on its own trajectory profoundly affecting their life choices.

And time does not heal -- it makes things worse. These children of divorce are subsequently presented with stepparents and stepsiblings, step dancing around every formerly happy family occasion. It's bewildering. In my own family it is extremely baffling. When my husband finally married that nice woman, she happened to be our son's mother-in-law. As my son put it, he went to bed with his wife and woke up with his sister. Like I said, 'Bewildering!'

After every big "D" divorce, birthdays, weddings and christenings can become tension–riddled events, and funerals are excruciating. Family dynamics take on the orderly course of a ten-car pileup on the Jersey Turnpike. Three families have been damaged -- his, hers and theirs -- and in "theirs" each member arrogates "most painfully afflicted" to himself. Families of divorce do not just veer off course, they get derailed.

Divorces involving long-term marriages have some commonality. Almost every woman who'd been divorced after a long marriage told me she never saw it coming. After decades with a husband you love (and they had loved them and often still did) there is a level of unquestioned trust. A radio interview I did with two young suburban ladies ended with one of them saying women like me must have been "out to lunch." A cruel and unfair judgment; we had marriages built on faith and reliance, entered into at a time when divorce was as unthinkable as it was unanticipated.

Many of the women I spoke with felt their husbands had hit an age when they had to face up to certain disappointments in their professional lives, and somehow transferred those disappointments to their marriage. Whereas, us wives had basic expectations that has been almost automatically fulfilled. My experience was typical of women married mid-twentieth century. We had children. We raised them. We'd have grandchildren. But men's expectations were different and not as easily met. No matter what occupation or profession they chose, they usually aimed at rising to the top. President. CEO. General. Chief of Staff. I bet 99.9 percent can't possibly meet their lofty goals and that's a bitter pill to be swallowed at their most vulnerable mid-life point, just when their children begin to leave home. Also leaving are their hair and teeth. Unfortunately, it all happens concurrently and catastrophically.

As much as I missed the children, like any mother whose chicks have flown the nest, my workload dramatically reduced. There was an upside. But their father missed their companionship, their looking up to him for guidance and advice, and at the same time he was being hit with whacking tuition bills. In every family there comes a time, when children change from being small persons looking up at their father with awe, to tall adults looking down on him making judgments. I believe absolutely that the empty nest syndrome is much tougher on men than women, and that midlife crisis is much more a male issue. Women may have hot flashes but men suffer a different kind of tormenting heat.

Another reality is that men are not always thrilled with the idea of being grandfathers. Catch the original movie of *Father's Little Dividend* and watch Spencer Tracy's reaction to the news that his daughter is pregnant. Or Jimmy Stewart's reaction in the wonderful *Mr. Hobb's Vacation.* My own father was a case in point. The arrival of my first baby

-- his first grandchild -- coincided with his fiftieth birthday and he had a full-blown, midlife crisis. Always heavyset, he went on a diet, popular at that time, eating only grapefruit. That was *all* he ate. He ate the pits and the rind. And when he'd lost sixty pounds, he celebrated by dying his white hair an alarming shade of orange. He informed me that when my child began to talk, he'd like to be referred to as, "Daddy John." I suggested that sounded like a laxative. He said he'd rather sound like a laxative than an old coot. Some men just have a tough time getting older. And forget altogether "mature." (My grandmother claimed there was no such thing as little girls, they're just short women. Conversely, there is no such thing as grown men, they're just tall boys.)

There are dozens of reasons couples divorce, but when a man in his fifties or sixties leaves his family, the common thread is his search for youth and freedom, and jettisoning his matronly wife can seem the perfect answer. Because when your life (especially your midlife) is not going well, the most natural thing in the world is to find someone to blame. Your mother or your spouse are the obvious choices, but you can't trade in your mother so it's Hobson's choice. Your spouse has to go.

One universal trait of men who bail out of long-term marriages is that they feel absolutely justified because of their wives' many failings. Their wives let them down and they themselves are nothing more or less than victims. Henry Ford once said of a colleague, "he took adversity like a man. He blamed his wife." In a catalog of menswear, I saw a T-shirt with a profoundly apt slogan, "I Didn't Say It Was Your Fault. I Said I Was Going To Blame You."

One of my dumped wife friends explained it flawlessly. She said if they came on television and announced, "tomorrow the world is coming to an end," her husband would have turned to her and said, "well now you've done it."

# CHAPTER 11
## Gedogen and Geezers

Why isn't there a feminine equivalent for the word *emasculate*? Because a career wife, whether widowed or divorced, after all those years feels "defeminized" without that man in her life. It's that feminine piece of your existence as half of a married couple that you mourn the most. I missed having a man in my life and in my bed. I missed having a date for every event -- a hand to hold -- a shoulder to lean on. And snuggling. I loved snuggling. I had lost my mate and my job and my income. Overnight the role of housewife (at which in all modesty I'd become quite accomplished) vanished because I no longer had anyone to keep house for. And without a husband, I couldn't be a wife either.

I had accepted as inevitable, that when my children became adults, I'd be marginalized as a mother. But I just couldn't imagine being a non-wife. I'd been stripped of the roles that defined my existence and forced to accept a position I'd never have optioned. I could not even say the word "divorcee." In my own mind I'd been "prematurely widowed" by a living husband. Think about it. Unless you're drafted into military service, almost every job you take in life has some element of free choice. So how can someone who doesn't even believe in divorce become a divorcee? Something I'd never contemplated and neither did my mother and her mother and all the mothers before me. What the hell is going on here?

One fact, reinforced by all the mail I received after my *New York Times'* article was published, was that most women being divorced by their husbands have had a much tougher going than I. My children were incredibly supportive and were adults so there were no custody or support issues. Unlike some wives whose husbands deserted them after they'd become ill or handicapped, I was in good health. I was truly blessed because for every person who let me down, two were there to prop me up. I was shaken to the core with disappointment when old friends cut me out of their lives and then warmed and encouraged by more casual friends who rallied round. But I was miserable.

As I mentioned, my husband had never been happier. The economist John Kenneth Galbraith has been credited with the observation that the happiest time in a man's life is right after his first divorce, and I believe it's true. Especially when that man married young, never having sowed his wild oats, and then finds himself totally free to explore exciting options. Which may be why older men who leave their older wives have an almost predictable structure to their breaking away, operating in accordance with the traditional Wife Abandonment Guidelines.

They move into "pads" (and actually call them that) and order stationery reflecting both their new addresses and new single status. They take up daring sports. One husband, whose only crack at a gold medal would have been if channel surfing became an Olympic event, took up skydiving and bought scuba gear. A friend's husband got a hat intended to make him look like Indiana Jones, but if truth be told, he looked more like the Frito Bandito. Being short, he wore cowboy boots with lifts and donned a safari jacket to go to his job into the wilds of Madison Avenue.

One guy I knew who was too macho to wear a wedding ring ("might as well put it through my nose") sported a diamond pinky ring. 'Shorty' with the cowboy boots also got a couple of big silver rings that looked like brass knuckles for Apaches. Often their entire wardrobe changes; goodbye Brooks Brothers, hello the Gap. Mutton trying to pass for lamb. A look so defined it's been assigned a name -- "Geezer Chic."

They trade in their big sedans for Porsches, which guarantee them lumbar problems, and they trade in their old wives for younger ones, which too can be hard on the back. Many a man who owes his success to his first wife owes his second wife to his success. I often want to say to a man or woman who breaks up a home and family, that just like in a gift shop, if you break it you own it. You must assume responsibility.

Unfortunately, we live in a society where many individuals refuse to assume accountability for their actions. They have good reasons and better excuses, and a tendency to minimize the effects of their actions. You see it everywhere -- people who bring thirty-three items to the express checkout lane or ride on the shoulder of the road to beat the traffic or park in the handicapped spaces, when, they're only handicapped by their own appalling lack of civility.

In the world I used to know, older couples didn't get divorced no matter what. My father was a larger than life original, but only a saint could have put up with him. My mother was that saint. Divorce was never an option for them, but when dad was especially kind and generous, mother used to admit, "I'm so glad I didn't murder him yesterday." Even a saint has temptations. No marriage is perfect but theirs was better than most. And far exceeded the glum expectation of the old country Irish that, "marriage combines the minimum privacy with the maximum loneliness."

When Steven Sondheim wrote *Company*, his definitive musical about commitment, the pivotal song on marriage was titled, *Sorry-Grateful*. If love is blind, marriage is a real eye-opener. It's said in the film community, that a wedding marks the end of the romantic comedy, and the marriage that follows becomes a documentary. It certainly becomes more of a drama. And the specter of divorce turns it into a melodrama. My own life segued from a fairytale to a soap opera to a 'Movie of the Week' on the WB channel. And finally, a Greek tragedy.

The one who can smile when things go wrong is the one who has thought of someone he can blame. So while the instigator of the divorce may be perceived by others to have traded responsibility and integrity for self-gratification and profligacy, he or she is personally devoid of guilt. And it helps that women, at least in my era, were primed to accept blame. We were fully responsible for the happiness of every member of our families. I remember apologizing profusely to my family because it was raining on a day we'd planned a picnic.

While the "victimized" spouse implementing his or her exit strategy feels little or no remorse, at variegated levels, everyone else involved feels guilt for all the shoulda, woulda, couldas. The family love that once nourished a child's self-esteem now sabotages it. Hopes, yearnings, traditions meant to be passed to the next generation, morph into booby-trapped heirlooms. Grown children can be more wounded than toddlers. Grandchildren get confused. Whatever benefit a couple receives from a divorce the undisputed fact is that their children will only be worse for it. In a big "D" divorce the collateral damage is staggering. It's Humpty Dumpty, where the pieces will never get put back together again.

A minister told me that in pre-wedding counseling, he always asks couples to define what would break the marriage contract, and they invariably say infidelity. They reject his suggestion that perhaps substance abuse or financial instability might present difficulties. But years later when they come back for desperately needed marriage counseling, fidelity is rarely the biggest problem.

So, here's where many of you who have stuck with this book up to now are going to send it sailing out the window. I believe there are only a very few valid reasons to break up a family, and infidelity is not one of them. Agatha Christie's *Miss Marple* solved many murders because of her knowledge of human nature, claiming that since she knew all about her neighbors in St. Mary Mead, she knew about the world. I have lived in a small village in the Hudson Valley for fifty years and have watched my neighbors live their lives. And I could (but I won't) name a dozen lovely families where the parents are celebrating golden anniversaries, although the husband had at least one flagrant and scandalous affair with another woman.

William Jones, the father of American psychology wrote, "wisdom is the art of knowing what to overlook." The Dutch have a word, "gedogen," which means turning a blind eye. My neighbors (plus several clever First Ladies) embraced these concepts, often pretending not to notice, and hung in there and kept their families intact. I see these couples now, enjoying their grandchildren, holding hands and caring for each other as infirmities of age crop up. I think how brave and unselfish these wives were, putting aside their own hurt and humiliation for the greater long range good of their families. And maybe themselves.

I believe that older women have been advising younger women on this subject through the ages. I recently saw a revival of the 1936 play, *The Women* by Claire Booth Luce (a smart cookie if ever there was one), where the lead character is urged by her friends to throw out her philandering husband while her wise mother urges her to hang in there. Eventually she follows her mother's advice and there's a happy ending.

I haunt flea markets and came across a book from 1909 titled, *The Journal of a Neglected Wife*. The first line from the wife reads, "Is he with her tonight?" and 253 pages later, the last line from the husband to his wife is "… the future would not seem so blank if I felt you were still with me. I have relinquished all right to your love, even to your pity. But … I hope you will stay." And she does, of course.

The conundrum posed always is, "but how can she ever trust him again?" Well some of these wives probably felt they could trust their husbands to bring home their paychecks, trust them to love their children as only a father can, trust them to keep their family safe and protected. And those were the "trusts" that they believed carried more weight than trusting them to keep their pants zipped.

We had neighbors in Brooklyn with eight kids, and the husband was a falling-down drunk whose children literally had to drag him home from the corner tavern almost every night. The family received welfare and all the neighbors tried to help the poor wife with food and second-hand clothes. When one of them finally asked her why she stayed with him, the wife replied earnestly, "because he never looks at another woman." That's what counted for her.

Years ago, my daughter was babysitting for a young couple going to a party. About midnight, the wife called me from a nearby town asking me to come and get her. Turned out, she'd caught her husband having sex with the hostess in the powder room and she'd panicked and ran from the house until she found a pay phone to call me. She was sobbing when I picked her up and said she wanted to kill herself. Halfway home she'd decided she wanted to kill him. By the time we reached her driveway, she decided what she really wanted was a BMW. Occasionally, I still see that woman driving through the village in yet another snazzy car and I wonder what her hubby has been up to. Basically each couple cuts their own deal, and picks the compromises they're willing to make.

A recent survey concluded that married women cheat for emotional support, while married men cheat for sex. Whatever the motive, adultery is wrong and disrespects both the spouse and the family. The "emotional support" piece is complicated but no one denies that men have strong sex drives … often more complex than women recognize. Husbands can be drawn to fetishes their wives can't comprehend. Or even imagine. So it can follow that a man who would never commit a malicious sin can be tempted to commit sins of the flesh.

Remember, in many stable societies, respectable married men are presumed to have mistresses. Which is a tough one. Having your husband go off the deep end after too many martinis at a convention is one thing. But it would be agonizing to know that your husband has another woman stashed away whose company he prefers. However, most times the guy returns home. He wants the excitement of a piece on the side. He doesn't want confrontation. He doesn't want the inconvenience of breaking in a new wife. He especially doesn't want to hurt his children. And if he's really smart, he'll recognize the self-defeating futility of ditching his wife for his girlfriend. Because God is a woman with a sense of humor who decreed that, human nature being human nature, A MAN WHO MARRIES HIS MISTRESS CREATES A JOB OPENING.

# CHAPTER 12
## Divorce as a Tsunami

A divorcee, like a widow, has to seriously reinvent her life when she becomes single. And the biggest help comes from friends. Most of mine were there for me and the ones that weren't, fit into the "Chinese/pizza" category. But the most encouraging were my fellow dumped wives. We rented *The First Wives Club* and enjoyed the movie even though the character we most associated with was Stockard Channing's (she jumped out the window in the first scene).

My own dismal experience aside, divorce by any standard is, the plague of our time. If the cornerstone of any stable society is the family, then a powerful movement that seriously weakens that structure is to be discouraged and fought off. As a middle-class woman, I have no personal experience with the profound problems divorce causes for the poor or the rich and would not presume to speak for them. Clearly, the financial and social pieces are very different. But the human quotient, the pain to children, has strong commonality.

*New York Times* columnist David Brooks, rightly claims that modern marriage is asked to survive in a culture of contingency -- of easily cancelled contracts. Why is it that, the most important contract you'll ever make, is the easiest to break? Try getting out of the contract for a car lease or a house purchase. It should be at least that difficult to get out of marriage where children are involved. Because (except in the most extreme circumstances) once you have taken on the spectacular obligation of having children, you should forfeit the right to a divorce if its only function is to place your happiness above theirs. A divorce, which will be the determining event in their lives, statistically sentences them to lifelong problems.

So often young couples today know more about pregnancy and childbirth than many physicians knew fifty years ago. They talk about ovulation and sperm count, trimesters and dilation and often have genetic tests preceding pregnancy. But do they realistically appraise their intended mate's ability to be a parent? Do they appreciate the importance of providing their baby with a stable home? Do they consider the scathing statistics on how deeply their child would be wounded by divorce? Couples with young children have enormous logistical problems as well as the financial ones, and must find their way among all the challenges incumbent on breaking up a family without fracturing its members.

Divorce doesn't have a ripple effect. It's more like a tsunami, uprooting everything in its path. The halcyon days of family harmony are over, replaced by discord, hurt feelings and bewildering alliances. Chaos would be a step up. And each family member hurts in a different place. The couple involved usually agree on nothing, starting with what one sees as desertion, the other views as leaving the scene of an accident. Ambient acrimony between the sexes is nothing new. Neither is adultery. Human nature can be a huge driving force. But what makes me cringe, along with hundreds of women who wrote to me, is when an unfaithful husband blames and disrespects his wife, especially if she is also the mother of his children. On this subject, back in 1921 Emily Post wrote, "a man who publicly besmirches his wife's name, besmirches more his own and proves that he is not, was not and never will be, a gentleman."

Divorce provides the ultimate Law of Unintended Consequences. People who seek a big "D" divorce don't usually set out to wound anyone but their spouses. They rarely think ahead to the collateral damage. In divorces, there are no winners. Everyone loses something. Everyone pays a price and often the departing husband and father pays a high price for a cheap piece. As one of my friends said about her brother's second wife, "you've heard of things money can't buy. She wasn't one of them." We always referred to that trophy wife as "the suicide blonde" (dyed by her own hand). Meow.

I am absolutely convinced that most parents contemplating divorce have not explored the potential cost to their children or themselves. It might be euphorically gratifying for a wife who's discovered her husband's infidelity to pitch his clothes out onto the front lawn and call a shark divorce lawyer. Or for a cuckolded husband to attempt to take custody of his children and cut off his wife financially. But neither of them have seized the moral high ground or acted in the best interest of the children. Most often they've simply decided that they'd rather be right than be happy. And this, unfortunately, is usually most devastating for women.

The numbers change every year, but substantially a divorced man sees his income rise by as much as fifty percent, while a divorced woman's income decreases by that or more. One of the most poverty-stricken groups in today's society is older, divorced women, who ultimately, become a burden to social services. So I have an idea to reform divorce law. Make it like damage to automobiles. No fault. None of this ridiculous "irreconcilable differences." I propose Pejorative Alimony to be imposed on any man who sees it as his right to abandon a long-time wife who stuck with him through thick bills and thin soup, and who has almost no chance to snag herself another mate.

In childless marriages, divide the assets. In decades-long marriages with children, the working wife gets three percent of her husband's income for every year difference between her age and the age of the woman he leaves her for. The stay-at-home wife with no means of support gets five percent, meaning a ten-year age difference will cost her ex fifty percent of his income. A twenty-year differential wipes him out completely. Forget marriage counselors, couples will be kept together by their accountants. How many younger women would want these older men if they came burdened with sexually transmitted debt?

These husbands would be better off in the long run. Younger wives of older men can stir up a lot of trouble. When you see a high-profile businessman or politician indicted, check the newspaper picture. How often have you seen a matronly wife by her accused husband's side? It's those sleek high-maintenance trophy wives who get guys into trouble. And they are usually very sleek. One of the AFGO husbands left with a young woman who looked like a stick figure. (My Irish grandmother would have said, "there's more meat on a butcher's apron.")

In days of yore, the typical deserting husband left his wife for a chippy like a chorus girl. But times have changed. Now older men often leave their wives for "superdames," professionally accomplished middle-aged sex bombs who've made bimbos obsolete. That is why these guys see them as their trophies, because usually they not only have less mileage on them than the first wives, but have more imposing curriculum vitae. Which just drives another knife into an old wife's heart. Bad enough her husband dumped her, but whereas she never climbed higher than Recording Secretary of the local Democratic Committee, her replacement is a State Senator, and, worse yet, a Republican. If she was a nurse, her replacement will likely be a thoracic surgeon, and so it goes.

In my little AFGO group, all our husbands traded up, but we got consolation from the spin our Afro-American friend Randreta put on this. She always referred to those trophy wives as Hoochie Mamas. When you know you're going to run into your ex and his spiffy new girlfriend it helps that you don't have to face, "there he is with the size six pediatric cardiologist." Instead what pops into your head is, "oh there's the Hoochie Mama," and you can tell your friends, "yes, Harry was there with his Hoochie Mama." It makes her seem less successful … less "the winner." It helps too, to remember that she may have his attention and his money, but you had him when he had his own teeth and hair. And plumped up in the right place.

You got to carry his children. She'll get to carry his denture adhesive. You got to organize his exciting first business. She'll get to organize his prostate treatments. And if, as often happens, she decides to have his baby, that baby won't be out of diapers long before her husband is in them. And since statistically second marriages have a higher failure rate than first marriages, the future of that union isn't always bright. Especially if the bride came down the aisle clutching a bouquet wrapped in a pre-nup agreement.

Up until the 1970s and '80s, in all history, marriage contracts were unheard of unless they involved succession to a throne. In some cultures there were dowries … upfront incentives for husbands in the "when" category. They've been replaced by pre-nuptial agreements -- aftermath incentives for husbands and wives in the "if when" category.

But for us common folk, when we took our vows, the marriage contract was implied. The husband would work to support the family and the wife would keep his house, cook his meals and tend to their children. If other conditions were set, they were more along the line of, if we go to your parents for Thanksgiving we'll have to go to mine for Christmas. Very little else required negotiation in those simpler times, when marriage was more safety net than tightrope. Now, especially with second marriages where the bloom is off the proverbial rose, we see marriage contracts so complicated that all they really guarantee is full employment opportunities for lawyers.

Because no matter how watertight your marriage contract is, it cannot guarantee a happy ending. Once upon a time never comes again. And no one lives happily ever after. George Kaufman once urged Irving Berlin to get real and reword his popular song *Always* so that it went, *"I'll Be Loving You … Tuesday."*

# CHAPTER 13
## Send in the Clowns

Jack and I had a favorite song, Sondheim's *Send In The Clowns*, and it ultimately became prophetic for several reasons. One line was particularly prescient ... *"I thought that you'd want what I want. Sorry my dear."* I sang that one more than a few times. The title originated in circus lore, inasmuch as when there is a tragic catastrophe and the Ring Master has to distract the audience, he calls out, "send in the clowns." If there were three places I never dreamed I'd find myself, they were Al-Anon meetings, divorce court, and, the unemployment office. But in my sixties I hit them all ... the trifecta of disappointments. Total desolation. Send in the clowns!

The one positive experience was Al-Anon, which is a twelve-step program for persons trying to deal with alcoholics in their lives. It is big on not being an "enabler" and teaches a valuable lesson in life. Because good people often, with the best motives and love in their hearts, enable (aka allow or encourage) those they love to behave badly. If we make excuses for our spouses, allow our children to postpone maturity, and our parents to become overly dependent, ultimately, we're not doing them any favors.

Another valuable precept of Al-Anon is that only children can be victims. Adults are volunteers. This is particularly apt when thinking about children of divorce, which also falls under that Law of Unintended Consequences. I've never known any parent who deliberately set out to hurt his or her child. But a mother who leaves her family to pursue her own goals, or follow a cute guy out the back gate, faces a hidden cost that is incalculable. So does the father who leaves his family to run after a more carefree lifestyle. Their children will probably always love them, but they might never respect them again.

Children, even grown ones, tend to lionize their fathers and idolize their mothers. I have seen mature men and women convulsed with grief at the loss of a dreadful parent because, whatever else, he or she was always there. There were no abandonment issues and no overtly embarrassing liaisons. A parent's death is always a defining moment for a child of any age. Essentially most of us who depart Planet Earth leave behind only one meaningful heritage ... the affection and respect of our children and grandchildren. Since you can't take anything with you, your life gets measured by what you left behind, and not primarily the tangible things, but the legacy that survives in the hearts and minds of your children. That bequest is precious and fragile but is rarely taken into account by a parent walking out the door on his or her family.

Next to wanting their own space, the divorce excuse I distrust the most is, "I want to find myself." Because a recent survey showed that in eighty-seven percent of actual cases, profound self-knowledge is not transporting. It's actually disappointing. Nevertheless, a woman I knew some years ago deserted her husband and teenage children to find herself. I grant you she was lost, but not the way she saw it. When I asked her how her kids felt about her leaving, she said, "all my children want is for me to be happy." I suggested she call Ripley. Because I'd never heard of a child whose first concern was a parent's happiness. I have great kids, but until well into their adulthood, they neither noticed nor cared if I was happy. I used to think that if they came home from school and found me unconscious on the kitchen floor they'd say, "does this mean dinner will be late?"

Bringing a child into this world is a magnificent responsibility. And in the best of worlds, adults don't create children as much as children create adults. It can be an amazing transformation. New parents often experience instant maturity and realigned priorities. Having children does not mean that you automatically forfeit the right to personal happiness, but you do forfeit the right to take it at their expense. Phyllis McGinley wrote that, "the hearts of the young are as brittle as glass." Forget harsh words, they can be wounded by a glance. A happy childhood is the best apprenticeship for adulthood. Conversely, no child completely recovers from a mangled childhood. A parents' divorce is such a harsh blow, except in the rare instance when the parents actually put the welfare of their children first.

Unfortunately, I've mostly seen the hostility between parents tear their children apart. Withholding child support may be the only way a man can control and hurt his ex-wife. Interfering with a father's visitation may be the only way an ex-wife can sock it to her ex-husband. The children they both love, all too often become pawns in an ugly game that no one wins.

A child of divorce usually has to deal with stepparents and stepgrandparents and stepsiblings. There was a picture in our local paper of a kindergarten graduate with his eight grandparents. By his high school graduation, relatives may be joined by his tutors, mentors, SAT coaches and admissions advisors, and too often, his drug counselor and conflict resolution coach. Because statistically, these children will have appalling problems.

This is not a book about statistics. (I hate them. I always think of them in my head as 'sadistics'.) But to fully recognize the crushing impact of divorce on children, I had to investigate them and they were worse than I'd imagined. With children of divorce living apart from their dads, only one child in six averages a weekly visit, and a decade after parents break up, two-thirds of their children have lost contact with their father.

Statistically, twenty to twenty-five percent of children of divorce are at risk for lifelong emotional or behavioral problems, compared to ten percent of those whose parents stay married. Those are worse odds than the association between smoking and cancer. Overcoming divorce is a painful struggle for young children whose parents usually underestimate those costs. And the emotional drain on adult children is as grave as it is incalculable.

In his groundbreaking book, *Mismatch,* Andrew Hacker observes that, "the motive of any divorce is to make life pleasanter for one or both of the adults, not to benefit the children (who) told their parents are going to part ... are given a burden they will carry for the rest of their lives. Put very simply, a grave reduction in the overall happiness of our nation's children has occurred, due to the decisions of their parents to divorce."

Often when the father remains in contact, the children can be even more miserable. One teenaged child of divorce told me, "I haven't seen my original father in years. Because the man who used to be my dad has morphed into Candi's boyfriend." I cringe at the self-delusion of men who explain that their daughters just love their new stepmothers, "they're like sisters." Children tolerate their parents' new spouses because they haven't got much choice, but it's rare that it goes further than that. It's difficult for children to accept a good stepmother when their own mother is dead. It's tantamount to impossible when their own mother is home crying her eyes out.

I would not dismiss the pain to children when their mother finds a new mate. Ideally, she would choose a man who cared for her children, but it's more likely a new husband will resent the time and energy she gives to children who are not his -- who resist his advice and resent his interference. If he also has children by a former marriage, the mix can be lethal. The Brady Bunch painted a rosy picture but the reality is thornier.

For heaven's sake, when a parent remarries, he or she should probably leave the children out of it. I wouldn't push for your son to be the best man or your daughter the maid of honor. In the most amicable divorces there is too much baggage. I've known many children who found it hard to handle the remarriage of their long-widowed parent, so when you add an angry abandoned parent who's been left behind, the accumulated pain can be crushing.

Recently, at a charity event, making conversation, I asked a young mother about her children. She gave me more detailed information than I wanted, and then said the most incredible thing. "I'll be so glad when they grow up and I don't have to worry about them anymore." I went straight to the bar. My grandmother (and probably yours) always said, "small children, headaches, grown children, heartaches." And I don't know any mother who is capable of being happier than her least happy child.  So it's in her own enlightened best interests to see to it that her children grow up as contented as possible. Which may, in her mind, justify overlooking her husband's failings and indiscretions, rather than subject her children to the ravages of divorce.

Now I have to backtrack because there are instances where divorce is the only answer, especially when there is abuse. Marriage without love often turns into love without marriage. But there are parents who handle divorce well. I have two close women friends who are second wives and stepmothers, and handle their roles with remarkable grace. And if they don't have the unconditional love of their stepchildren, they do have their respect and affection. They encourage their husbands to meet privately with their children and to keep in touch with them and support them in every way. They never say an unkind word about their husband's former wife to anyone, no matter how tempted. One of these second wives told me that she couldn't love her husband unconditionally if he didn't put his children first. And so her most fortunate husband never feels torn between his children and their stepmother, and everyone is better for it.

There is a cosmic difference between children who feel the pain of loss when a parent died and those whose parent deserted their homes ... and, too often, them. Trust erodes. Children who sense abandonment feel separated from that parent by yards of thin ice. So it's not just the booby who gets trapped. My friend's five-year old grandson had had his lifestyle dramatically downsized when his dad, after promising that he would always be there for him, completely abandoned the family. Last Christmas, his grandmother took him to see Santa, who assured the child he'd make sure his wishes came true. Santa said, "you can trust me on that." And the little fellow, as he slid off Santa's lap, asked, "but are you and your wife getting along?"

# CHAPTER 14
## Age and the "Tiger"

On her seventieth birthday, my Aunt Florence was asked if sex ended at seventy, and she said, "no, forty." And she meant it. Poor Uncle Fred. If there is sex over seventy, I have no firsthand experience, mores the pity, I guess. A couple of years ago, on a foray into Tijuana with my grandchildren, I watched a steady parade of geezers hobbling into the Farmacias to buy over-the-counter Viagra (known to my AFGO group by the more generically correct name, 'Mycoxafloppin'), while their wives sat on sidewalk benches with expressions on their faces usually reserved for doomed souls being hauled away in tumbrels headed for the guillotine.

I read recently that there's more money being spent on breast implants and Viagra than on Alzheimer's research, which probably means that before long, there should be a large older population with perky breasts and big erections and not a clue what to do with them.

However, on the plus side of septuagenarian sex, I do have a hopeful anecdote. My lawyer husband was the judge in our village, which gave him the privilege to perform weddings. So when a widowed client asked that he marry her to a fine widower, I invited them to have the ceremony in our home where I could provide a proper wedding reception for their immediate families. The bride was a sturdy Swedish woman in her early seventies, the groom a few years older. To make conversation as we toasted them with champagne, I asked how they met.

I was *so* sorry I asked. The groom went into a protracted story. They were staying at the same apartment complex in Florida and he asked her if she'd go to a motel with him. She asked when. He gave her a date a few days off, and then explained that the motel he had in mind had special black lights in the bedrooms, and if she would wear white satin underwear it would be very stimulating. He went into rather graphic details about this excitement and I was mortified. I couldn't look at the bride. My God she must be humiliated. But when the groom wound up his wide-ranging description of the motel setting, the bride cheerily piped up in that charming Swedish singsong, "and ever since that night he calls me Tiger."

Tiger's enthusiasm for sex was unanticipated, although, like most celibate seniors, I look back fondly at my love life, and occasionally despair that it's so over. There was a darling gay man who had a shop in our village and a very old lady (90+), helped him in the store just to get out every day. When he decided to close up and move to Florida I said to the woman, "I bet you're going to miss Harold." She said, "yes, Mrs. Hekker I really am, because every morning when I come in, he asks me if I got laid last night. And once he's gone, no one will ever ask me that again." *I know the feeling.*

An elderly gentlemen in my family asked me to come to his Senior Club to check out a lady who had indicated she'd like to get closer to him, and who met his number one criteria -- she could drive at night. Since his own eyesight was failing, my job was to tell him if she was very wrinkled. Naturally I asked if he couldn't see the wrinkles what was the difference, but he claimed he had a reputation in the senior community and would not be seen with a really crumple-faced lady. Her face was like seersucker, but I assured him you could hardly tell her from Julia Roberts. On another front, a year ago when one of my friends remarried in her mid-seventies, she merrily confided to all, that her revived sex life hinged on her new husband's ability to keep the weight on his elbows. That was a lot more than anyone needed to know.

Often, diminished sex lives notwithstanding, as you hit your mid to late sixties you are barraged with losses and infirmities. Losing your eyesight and hearing, your hair, your siblings and friends. Knees creak and your hands can't open the childproof cap on your arthritis pills. And that's the good news. Because the bad news about old age is that you didn't make it. John Mortimer wrote that, "no one should grow old who isn't ready to appreciate the ridiculous."

I have chosen to view advanced age as a gift. Legitimately no American has died of old age since 1951 when the government dropped that official cause. Which fits right in with my old Irish family view that illness must be denied at all costs. Which explains how one of my grandfather's brothers died of "nothing serious" and another succumbed to "shortness of breath." When asked what his sister died of, grandpa said, "she died of a Tuesday."

Also old age has been seriously redefined. Today, sixty-four year olds can expect to live sixteen more years. In her writings about life's passages, Gail Sheehy claims that eighty-four is the new sixty-four. And like almost all my contemporaries, I never think of myself as old, although I can't reconcile that my grandmother's hands are sticking out of my sleeves.

As for living alone, I love it. It is, like age, liberating. You have nothing left to prove. No one left to impress. No burdensome responsibilities. You don't need permission from anyone for anything. If you are fortunate enough to have good health and enough money to pay your bills, these can be the best years of your life.

First you're pushing fifty, then sixty, then seventy. Then you begin pushing your luck. The one word answer to a happy old age is ACCEPTANCE. Complaining about your infirmities is useless. And worse, boring. I don't ever say, "I'm too old to ..." because most often that's not even true. I just don't want to do that any more. The other phrases I try not to say are, "In my day ..." or "I remember when..." or "what's the matter with kids today?" Because there's nothing the matter with kids, although there are some things wide of the mark with parents.

Grandchildren are a great gift. Fountains of youthfulness in an otherwise arid landscape. I believe the prospect of old age and dying must be harder for people without grandchildren bringing new and exciting events into a life otherwise bursting with losses. My father had a theory that the great bond between grandparents and grandchildren is that they have a common enemy. In my experience this is not the case, although it seems young couples today take parenthood dramatically more seriously than we did.

Parenthood has gone from a natural obligation to a cult. A friend was told, that like all the guests at the rather extravagant christening party for his grandson, he was not to go into the nursery (germs you know) but could view the baby through a special glass door. He reminded his daughter-in-law that he was a pediatrician. She was unmoved. He pressed his nose against the glass like everyone else. And his experience was not that far ahead of the curve.

When grandparents get together they almost always bemoan the fact that their children don't believe in playpens. Instead, today's parents childproof their homes to the point that when you visit, you can't open a cupboard door or plug in an appliance. And caring for your grandchild is not for the technically challenged. I have never mastered the intricacies of the car seat and I can't coax the stroller to fold or unfold. While I've developed a strong attachment to SpongeBob SquarePants, Barney and Telletubbies make my sinuses ache.

A cynic said that parenthood is the unprepared attempting the impossible for the sake of the ungrateful. I believe being a mother is the highest calling a woman can have, and disagree with that assessment, especially the "unprepared" part. Today's parents are usually over-prepared and they are certainly better equipped … often with designer diaper bags and Burberry car seats and $900 strollers. They have barbaric breast pumps and agonize over using a supplemental bottle for fear of causing their babies 'nipple confusion.'

Forget rattles, their infants have Baby Einstein and Baby Bach to amuse and enlighten them, and women leaving the corporate world for full-time mothering often hire transition coaches. My grandmother O'Donohue was the best mother I ever knew because she loved her children deeply and unconditionally. She never read one book about parenting and was so uninformed about the process that when my mother told her she was having a hysterectomy and that her uterus would be removed, grandma inquired if that would make it more difficult for her to get pregnant.

And if you don't think parenting is getting more status driven, go to a toddler's birthday party. What ever happened to pin the tail on the donkey and cupcakes with candles? How did children's birthday parties become *events*? With themes and hired entertainers. I dropped in on my grandson's fifth birthday party and was met by a python and an iguana right out of a Japanese horror movie. The theme was "Exotic Animals." I almost had an exotic coronary.

One evening a group of my friends, all grandparents, had a discussion about life, and after a few glasses of wine the subject of death came up, and someone threw out the question of what you'd do if you learned you had only one more year to live. There followed a series of philosophical ideas mostly involving churchgoing and works of mercy. Until the most serious and scholarly man there, came up with this profound concept. "I'd spend it going to children's birthday parties, because every minute would seem like an hour and at the end of the year I'd be happy to die." He nailed it!

My children, God bless them, never ask me to babysit for anyone younger than five. I do well with infants ... they can't go anywhere. And there's something about a baby's breath on your neck that fills your heart. But running after toddlers as they careen toward the stairs or put pins in their mouths makes me crazy. I've talked this over with grandmothers who had big families themselves and they share my feelings. Having multiple babies/toddlers at once is an experience we want to put behind us. And faced with reliving it, we're like people once kidnapped by terrorists who now can't handle a cellar door closing behind them. We suffer terrifying flashbacks.

For all the griping people of my generation do about kids today and how we did things in the good old days, the truth is today's parents do a great job. I came from a very loving family, but I can assure you that neither my father nor grandfather ever read a bedtime story to his children. Nor did my husband. My father never went to one of our school plays or sporting events -- he had to be blackmailed into going to our graduations. My sons spend more time with their children than their father did, and however our marriage ended, I have to say when they were young, he was a very attentive parent.

Sometimes I believe today's fathers are a little too conscientious. I occasionally think my sons got more out of playing pick-up baseball games in the empty lot across the street than my grandsons get playing organized little league. But I love that my granddaughters are playing team sports and that every child is encouraged to maximize his or her strengths. I certainly learned discipline and values in Catholic schools but they were short on individual attention, in a time when a small class had upwards of fifty children being kept in line by one small nun (albeit with the intimidation powers of a panzer division).

One fact that clouds our vantage point is, that as our children generally marry later than we did, we tend to come to grandparenthood at a more advanced age. My mother became a grandmother at forty-two. I first became a grandmother at fifty-six and was seventy-one when the last one was born. When I see women in their fifties having babies or men in their seventies fathering them, I wonder if they have totally lost their minds.

Generally speaking, grandparents who are over sixty should not be expected to babysit unless they insist. Over sixty-five, if they insist, but no overnighters. Over seventy, don't even think about it. They want to help. They'd give their lives for those kids. But it's too much to ask them to assume responsibility for small children. As a general rule, grandparents should not be expected to take responsibility for children more than sixty years younger than they are.

Certainly the last decades of life are more complicated than the previous ones. You have been someone. You've been loved and hated (sometimes by the same person). You have probably been left alone. But age is a gift not a burden. My mother died at fifty-one without seeing most of her grandchildren, so I would be ungrateful to complain about the failing eyes and creaking knees of later life. I honestly see every day a gift.

There are no fixed rules about aging. The only tenet I absolutely adhere to, is that when someone offers you a breath mint, take it. And it probably falls under the category of cognitive dissonance that while fully conscious of their age, most elderly people continue to look ahead, often convinced the best is yet to come. When Ruth Gordon won an Academy Award at seventy-two, she said, "I can't tell you how encouraging a thing like this is."

What amazes me about my contemporaries is that, we are all so cheerful, although facing the inevitability of approaching death with its attendant suffering and mortification. Most of us treasure each day even though there's little good news in the newspaper and none at all in the mirror. But there are bright moments. P.G. Wodehouse said, "the great privilege of becoming an octogenarian is that you are no longer expected to go to parties. The thought that I shall never have to wear a party hat again is sustaining."

I lean toward Woody Allen's vision of death. He said, "I don't want to achieve immortality through my work. I want to achieve it by not dying." Nevertheless one of my favorite stories about someone reaching the end of the road is told about the great playwright Lillian Hellman by her friend, Peter Feibleman. She was seventy-nine when he went to visit and her nurse told him that, "Miss Hellman is paralyzed, blind and having some rage attacks … as the result of her strokes. She can't sleep. She can't eat … her memory is beginning to fade and … frankly … she's dying." Peter thanked her for the heads up and went in to Lillian asking, "how are you?" "Not good," Lillian said, "this is the worst case of writer's block I've ever had. *The* worst case."

# CHAPTER 15
## Marriage on the Rocks

In November 1954, the unthinkable happened. Our family was rocked by scandal. My Irish aunt was marrying an Italian man. The shock wave resonated through our Brooklyn parish and although they were both devout Catholics, the Irish pastor of our church balked at performing this "mixed marriage" ceremony. Given the rocky start, there was a happy ending -- they had seven terrific children and their grandson sat in the United States Congress.

My girlhood friend Mary Ann, the beautiful teenage daughter of Italian-born parents, fell in love with an Irish lad and her parents relocated to break them up. Twenty-five years later, both divorced, they met again, married and celebrated their 25th wedding anniversary. By the time they finally married, the Irishman, the adorable and talented Charles Durning, was a very successful actor and Mary Ann's parents moved in with them in Hollywood. Another happy ending!

I was told that my grandmother's sister married a Jew in the 1920s and they died in one of the first fatal automobile accidents in New York State which, the story goes, seemed only fitting given the way they flaunted convention. Marriage between two races was a crime (called miscegenation) in several states until the mid-twentieth century.

I never even dated a guy who wasn't Irish Catholic. Although my husband carried the last name of a Dutch grandfather, his other three grandparents were Irish born. And I now have five children, only one of whom was married in a Catholic church. Eight of my extraordinary 12 grandchildren have Jewish ancestors. That would have been unimaginable only five decades ago. The point is, everything about marriage is changing. Religious and ethnic barriers are all but invisible and we're all better for that.

When I married in the 1950s, and for thousands of years before, marriage was the destination of choice for every female child. The traditional, historic marriage as spelled out about 1750 B.C. in the Code of Hammurabi, and reinforced by subsequent common law, did not address 401K plans, health insurance, green cards or pension benefits. Marriage through the centuries was primarily a civil contract that would protect children and property rights.

The Catholic Church didn't even make it a sacrament until 1215. In every faith it became a lifetime commitment with some variation of "till death us do part" in the ceremony. A married couple was two people committed to a lifetime of caring for each other and nurturing their children within the framework of a family. Why has there been so much press about gay marriage and so little consideration given to the primary reason marriage itself was originally conceived? The protection of children.

The American Community Survey released in the fall of 2006 by the Census Bureau, found that less than fifty percent of households are now made up of married couples. A growing number of adults are living their lives single or shared with unmarried partners, which changes the social weight of marriage in the economy and in how we set up work policies. Further indicating the changing face of matrimony.

As mentioned earlier, up until the middle of the twentieth century, marriage contracts had implied conditions. He will support her and their family financially, and she will care for his home and bear his children. In this twenty-first century, the evolutionary process has taken us to a place where women don't need men to protect and support them, or even to impregnate them. Men don't need women to tend their nests and cook their meals (think cleaning services and Stouffer's). And, the way cloning is headed, they won't need them to bear their children either. So we are on the brink of a very new stage in all marriages -- relationships built on wanting instead of needing -- based not on dependence but on mutual independence, and respect paired with undefined and to-be-negotiated roles.

I was recently reminded of the old saying that, 'marriage is the price men pay for sex, and sex is the price women pay for marriage'.

There's a Wife's Prayer which goes, "Dear Lord, I pray for wisdom to understand this man, to love and forgive him and for patience with his moods, because Lord if I pray for strength, I'll just beat him to death." On balance, there's the husband's line about never realizing what true happiness was until he got married and then it was too late.

Putting aside all that cynicism, the thing is, marriage itself is just not what it used to be. What the Supreme Court called "a sacred obligation" in the nineteenth century was referred to as "an association of two individuals" by 1965. And by 2003, the institution of marriage is impossible to delineate. James Q. Wilson in his *The Marriage Problem* says there is more "I Don't" than "I Do" in these loose confederations. More than half of marriages end in divorce, and as marriages are sliced and diced, there is the inevitable diaspora of family and friends. And God help the children.

The forthcoming edition of the *Oxford English Dictionary* will define *marriage* as the "legal or religious union of two people." The meaning of *family* is changing too. The 1992 *American Heritage Dictionary* defined family as, "a fundamental social group consisting of a man, a woman and their offspring." The 2000 edition altered the definition to, "typically consisting of one or two parents and their children."

In a world where there is so much hate, why quibble about legally recognizing the union of two people who love each other? In the early 1990s I wrote a piece for our local Chamber of Commerce brochure that got me into hot water. It boasted that Nyack was a small village but cosmopolitan in its makeup, and that it was the only village in the Hudson Valley where couples strolled the downtown holding hands. Often those hands were different colors or belonged to persons of the same sex, but that's what made our town special. Several years later, as mayor, I proposed and we passed, the first domestic partnership law in our county, giving benefits and rights to unmarried partners.

Because our community, which was historically multi-racial welcomed diversity, we have a good number of same-sex families, and they and their children are comfortable here. As they should be everywhere. I am blessed to be involved with the lives of my young grandchildren, and I see little difference in the devotion to their children among my same-sex neighbors and the heterosexual ones. Loving couples who give their children safe and nurturing homes are to be encouraged, particularly same-sex couples who often adopt children otherwise destined to be shuffled from one foster home to another. So let's not fret about the sexual orientation of couples getting married and instead concentrate on how we can make these unions strong enough to support and cherish the children who may come into them.

While our government has considered spending $1.5 billion to promote marriage, the more pragmatic European countries are moving in the opposite direction, providing mechanisms for couples who wish to formalize their alternative relationships. France offers a "Civil Solidarity Pact" and Portugal and Holland offer "Partnership Rights" and "Registered Partnership" to both hetero and homosexual couples. Denmark and Germany offer "Registered Partnership" to same-sex couples.

There is a new-fangled word, retronym, which indicates a noun that only recently required an adjective. (Example "oven" which can now be prefixed by "toaster," "convection," "microwave," etc.) Like it or not, marriage now comes in many forms and often requires an adjective. Trial marriage, open marriage, same-sex marriage. The times they are a-changing, but what has not changed is the deep need for children to have loving parents and stable homes. And if we fail to recognize that fact, we are doomed to future generations of unhappy and unproductive adults.

Soon after my first book was published, I was invited to participate in a round-table panel on sex roles at a local college. I confined my opinions to women's issues but a discussion of sexual preferences began. There were heated arguments about whether homosexuals could have their orientation changed by therapy. The discussion was on such a high level, I didn't understand some of the big words and couldn't follow the convoluted theories on what forms our sexual preferences. But everything was finally put in perspective by an elderly family doctor on the panel who shouted out, "for God's sake, you can't even turn an ass man into a tit man." I've become convinced that what "turns you on" is deep-seated and inexplicable. How else can I explain my weakness for men with thick necks?

I do not understand homophobia. The gay people I know no more chose their lifestyle than they chose the color of their eyes. Should we discriminate against people with blue eyes? The gay members of our families want to belong. They want to love and be loved. And now there's all this flack about same-sex marriages and protecting traditional marriage, like traditional marriage is such a rousing success.

The critical measure of every issue in a democracy is justice and equality -- and acceptance for God's sake. If our Federal Government is so invested in preserving the sanctity of marriage, maybe they should make divorce illegal and brand adulterers. As a Catholic, I cringe at the Vatican's objection to gay couples adopting children because it might put those children "in harms way." Clearly cathedrals are not glass houses.

The Stanford linguist Geoffrey Nunberg wrote that the word *marriage* is more charged than most because it's what is called a "performative notion." That is, a state of affairs that can be brought about merely by pronouncing certain words. He argues that opponents of gay marriage may feel that it will threaten the institution of marriage itself because it's like "opening up an exclusive hotel to package tours with the risk that the traditional clientele will no longer feel like checking in."

When I was mayor, I performed dozens of weddings for couples who showed up in front of me with valid licenses from the State. As far as I could tell, (sometimes it wasn't easy), they were opposite-sex couples, but few had romance on their minds. One rather desperate older woman married a man on his three-hour pass from a mental hospital, and when the union didn't work out it was my fault. She had once shouted at me across Main Street, "you ruined my life."

Several marriages were prompted by green card issues, but my most bizarre was a couple where the groom could not have been more rude and grumpy. I suggested he take a seat while I completed the forms, but he refused and just paced and squirmed. The bride finally shared the problem with me. He needed to marry her to be able to access her health insurance to pay for the hemorrhoidectomy he was having the next day. And here I thought the guy standing in front of me was a perfect asshole. But not yet.

# CHAPTER 16
## Men and Women: Need and Want

Many of the women who wrote to me were suffering from fresh wounds, unable to imagine ever feeling contented again. When replying, I tried to convince them that they could look forward to joyful lives. It took time, but all of my dumped wives friends are happier and healthier than we were when our husbands first left. Affirming what Neitzeche said about what does not destroy us makes us strong. Not one of us has remarried, or wanted to. Face it, the only men who might want a woman in her sixties are in their eighties and looking for a nurse/housekeeper who'd work cheap, or a lady with money. What my friend Louise calls a nurse or a purse!

We didn't mind being alone, but we hated being divorced. Discarded. Dumped. Disgraced. Deleted. We felt we'd let down our children by not keeping their families intact. But we began to relish our freedom. Living alone has its bright side especially for someone like me who married from her parents' home and never had a taste of independence. I enjoy keeping terrible hours and sleeping in old T-shirts and the freedom of not having to report to anyone.

Going to parties alone takes guts, but on the plus side, you only have to worry about whether you're having a good time, and aren't constantly on the lookout for your spouse's "get me the hell out of here" signal. My husband once admitted, in a moment of exquisite candor, that the thing he treasured most about me was my willingness to continue conversations he'd long ago lost interest in. Like many men, he never got high marks in "listens attentively." Once at a dinner party, a guest took the floor to enumerate the sterling qualities of each of her six children, and when she finally, mercifully, finished, my husband asked, "so do you and your husband have a family?" I was the only one there who knew he wasn't kidding.

As mentioned previously, adult conversation is not the big selling point of many husbands, with whom most verbal discourse is more extraction than conversation. Television is a big part of the problem, especially sports, since commercials which once gave respite, are now an opportunity to surf the channels. My special gripe was when we were going someplace and my husband said we could leave as soon as the football game ended -- there were only a few minutes left in the game. Forty-five minutes later, I was still standing by the door with my coat on. The constant televised sports were the things I missed least about married life.

I did, however, terribly miss my children's father, the traditional head of our family. I missed the bicameral authority of the other parent when dealing with problems. Without the presence of that strong father there was often disarray and uncertainty. It's like when Tito died, he may not have been a benevolent dictator but he kept the country together and once he was gone, unimaginable confusion took hold. Eventually we all worked through the incomprehensible pain and, if anything, my children are now closer to me, and each other, than they were before the divorce.

It is a profound truth, that the most important thing a man can do for his children, is love their mother. Once that is gone, the entire family loses security and the wife loses companionship, that whole delightful man/woman thing. Affection and shared joys, not just sex. In that department, wives deserted by alcoholics get one clear advantage having already become used to conjugal hypothermia. It's not easy to light a fire under someone who's soggy. One distressed wife shared in detail, at an Al-Anon meeting, that booze ruined her sex life. Her memorable line was, "it would have been easier to raise the Titanic."

Eventually (it took a few years), I came to realize that my personal journey was part of a larger, more significant picture. Never having been trendy, I found myself, inadvertently, in the advance squad of a powerful new movement that was realigning all the gender-based relationships. Women used to rely on men for sex and heavy lifting but now men are being threatened not only by Women's Lib and Affirmative Action, but by artificial insemination and vibrators and luggage on wheels. Power tools have allowed women to enter fields once exclusive to stronger men. Less than a half-century ago, women doctors and lawyers were oddities. Women police and firefighters were non-existent. And there was only one way for a woman to become pregnant.

The astute economist Stanley Lebergott coined the phrase "men's liberation," to describe the freedom that enables husbands to leave their wives and children with little or no social censure. I'll drink to that! It was just one of the Unintended Consequences of Women's Liberation that gave added bonuses to men as it opened the door for sex before marriage, and, the shared paycheck afterwards. To say nothing of providing universal acceptance of the Dutch treat.

The changes are coming fast and furious and there's no going back and getting mushy over the good old days. No point in driving forward with our eyes firmly fixed on the rearview mirror. Grandma was one kind of mother. My mother was another. I am at a different place and the women after me will be even more diverse. But when a woman becomes a mother, she desperately wants what's best for her child, and the working mothers in my family are every bit as devoted and nurturing as their homebound grandmothers were. It's time to put aside all those debates on the working mother vs. the stay-at-home mother. It's as pointless as debating the horse and buggy vs. the automobile.

When I was called to be part of a panel on *Good Morning America*, the subject was, "The Mommy Wars," a phrase I deplore. I resent anything that pits women against women because we are, for the most part, each other's strengths. Women traditionally "tend and befriend." I don't believe these 'wars' really exist, except in the media. Every chance I get, I ask young mothers if, while staying home, they resent the ones who work and vice-versa, and not one answers yes. There is always the grass-is-greener factor -- watching your neighbor beautifully dressed and heading out to work in the morning might make a stay-at-home mother in sweatpants get wistful. The woman headed out on a cold morning might look longingly at her neighbor pouring herself a second cup of coffee. But when it comes to hostility I never found it. The mothers who work are grateful to their stay-at-home relatives and neighbors who often cover for them, and, the stay-at-home moms are usually rewarded by help with childcare on weekends.

An unanticipated and often unrecognized consequence of our shifting lifestyles is that as women leave the house for the workplace there has been a great burden placed on human care agencies. The more fragile members of a family -- the elderly and the disabled -- were traditionally cared for in the home by women. Without these caregivers, a heavy load has been placed on support agencies and this is a critical and often ignored corollary of our shifting lifestyles. Especially right now as budget crunches cut back on these government-sponsored programs.

In the inspiring book, *Compassion's Lure,* Kathleen Lukens said, "... those afflicted are a kind of lightning rod for a collective adversity that reassures those of us spared. If so, the bright, the beautiful and the blest owe something to the hapless and the hurt. In that sense, we are all each others gifts to one another." If a society is measured by how it cares for its most vulnerable members, then we'd better take a hard look at how our tax dollars are being prioritized.

Most people are like my grandfather O'Donohue, who proclaimed that he believed in progress, but he didn't like change. Change is uncomfortable and unsettling, but it is always less stressful if you've planned for it. Since there are now more women in colleges than men, it's likely that most young mothers will be out working or planning to go back to work. There should be no downside and no guilt in that as long as their children are well provided for. So let's get serious about better and more convenient daycare. Let building codes demand on-site childcare facilities in every large office building, in every mall. We've used these codes to provide for the needs of our physically handicapped. Are our children any less deserving?

I think we all would like to see universal health care for our children and safe, well-equipped schools. Making it easier (it will never be easy) for parents to support and encourage their children. And let's allow our children to be children. Take some of the crushing structure out of their after-school hours and limit the amount of books they can bring home each night to five pounds. I've threatened to run for President on a simple platform -- No Homework and Year-Round Daylight Saving Time. More time and light to play outside after school. It will capture the hearts of parents and grandparents across the land. I think it's a winner.

I came from a family that valued education. Because my father only had an eighth-grade diploma himself, he saw to it that my sister and I finished college, and that my four brothers obtained graduate degrees from Ivy League universities. But as seniors in high school, none of us had as much homework as my grandchildren have now in the third grade.

We live in a world that's shrinking and shifting so fast we're spinning. A world suddenly so small that there is nowhere you couldn't be tomorrow. Happenings at the furthest points on the earth shape our daily lives. Globalization means connection, for better or worse, and exposure to foreign ethical and moral standards. But from what I can tell, there is also a strong commonality among even the most exotic cultures, because essentially we are all defined by patterns formed long ago, forged through heredity and evolution. And all cultures, however exotic, share the central theme of love of family.

Family is the most defining and vital part of our lives. In New York City, the most cosmopolitan location in our country, the social life may seem to outsiders as one defined by *Sex and the City*. But after the tragedy of September 11, *The New York Times* ran obituaries of all those thousands lost, and every single one was about their ties to their families. Their last calls to wives, husbands, mothers and siblings. Their overriding concerns for loved ones mirrored in our own family's terror, because my youngest son Tommy was on the thirtieth floor of the North Tower and we frantically clung to each other for those long hours before he got out and was able to reach us.

Most people I know have admirable moral compasses. But it's getting harder and harder, because we live in a general society that can be slapdash, and a media that too often applauds and rewards aberrant behavior. I know that my mother invented the phrase, "no good deed goes unpunished," she said it long before it became a common mantra. But now we have, "no bad deed goes unrewarded," as people become celebrities for acts that in a less liberal time would have caused them to be flogged. Forget the spotted owl, the most endangered species today is the blackmailer, as people brag about actions which only a few years ago they'd have paid a fortune to keep quiet.

We live in an era where shallow people often seem to abound. Value systems have changed and not always for the better. Greed is now defined as "irrational exuberance." And whatever happened to guilt? It seems now only to apply to what we eat.

In the history of a world where hunger was and is the overriding problem, this obsession with weight is a relatively new phenomenon. Individuals will cheat on their taxes and their spouses. They'll use their positions in the business world to defraud their clients and employees, or use their positions in the political world to swindle the people who voted for them. And no problem. But if they cave in to an urge to eat a couple of Krispy Kreme doughnuts they're racked with remorse.

I have this vision of a woman who brings her children to an unreliable daycare center, then goes to her job selling defective smoke alarms. She spends her lunch hour in a motel sharing adulterous sex and a pizza with extra cheese with her boss. On the way home she shoplifts a small steak and a *TV Guide*, and when she goes to bed that night the only thing she feels guilty about is the extra cheese.

I am not immune from obsession with weight. I want the bumper sticker that says, "I wish I was as fat as I was in high school." When we were both sixteen, I met Elizabeth Taylor and spent the ensuing years praying to have her waistline. Well I finally have it. Be awfully careful what you pray for.

# CHAPTER 17
## Bite Your Éclair

I come from a family of talkers. Once at dinner my father shouted out, "shut up!" and we did. He continued, "there are nine people at this table and five of you are talking. One of you does not have a listener. Either pick up a listener or be quiet." He seemed oblivious to the reality that his six children had perfected the device of talking and listening simultaneously. And, to facilitate this and speed things up, we'd also developed some shortcuts -- phrases of a few words to indicate a more involved thought or idea. These phrases culled from memorable events in our young lives.

One Thanksgiving, our Aunt Katie took charge of bringing food to the children at the card table in the living room, and admonished us, "whatever you do don't put the peas up your nose." Well guess what the boys did the minute she turned her back? Ever since then, when the family was discussing a situation where you don't want to give anyone the wrong idea, our shorthand phrase was, "peas up your nose."

When faced with a problem that demanded action to achieve a serious priority, an entitlement, albeit a somewhat self-serving one, the phrase was, "take a bite of your éclair" which originated on the Sunday when, instead of a homemade dessert, our mother has splurged on eight éclairs. And just as we were about to eat them, the doorbell rang and we realized our parish priest was paying his Sunday visit. So the cry went out, "quick, take a bite of your éclair."

That phrase became our shorthand for look out for yourself, and first things first and priorities matter. It's been banging around in my head as I've researched books and articles about the sorry state of affairs of women, especially working mothers, in this country. Because I couldn't figure out why our Women's Liberation Movement, which was so successful in getting women equality of opportunity in education and business, didn't press on to deal with the needs of working mothers?

The courageous women who founded the Women's Movement recognized unconscionable gender injustice, and sought to rectify the problem. These predominantly well-educated, professional women took actions appropriate to the hurdles they faced while achieving political and social equality. As they tackled the most pressing problems and priorities, they took a bite of their éclairs and there's nothing wrong with that. My sainted mother bit hers. But those who came after them tragically dropped the ball.

The most recent statistics have women in the workforce making eighty-one percent as much as men (up from sixty-three percent in 1979) and that's progress. But even those numbers don't quite tell the story, because today for the first time, women in their twenties who work full-time in cities like New York, Boston and Chicago, are earning higher wages than men in that age group. Probably because thirty-six percent of female workers now in their twenties have a college degree, compared with twenty-three percent of males.

Regarding the efficacy of the Women's Movement, in his book, *The Decline of Males,* the renowned anthropologist Dr. Lionel Tiger wrote, "events have far overtaken the boldest expectations … Millions of years of evolutionary regularity have been altered in a very brief period." But to mix metaphors, their revolution caught on like wildfire then overshot the runway. Maureen Dowd nailed it writing that, "feminism lasted for a nanosecond, but the backlash has lasted forty years."

Ms. Dowd was an inspiration to me because as a very bright and independent professional woman, she comes from a very different place than I, and yet exposed the same problems. Especially when she referred to the writer Nina Burleigh, who wrote in *The New York Observer,* that it was depressing to see women trying to patch up their dignity after their men took off with younger more pliant females. That, "feminism wasn't supposed to mean brokenhearted women in middle age."

There is a great deal to be grateful for that came out of the Feminist Movement. I am personally thankful that, in 1994, with barriers lowered, I could become the first woman mayor of my hometown. And I'm grateful that my eight granddaughters have, thanks to Title IX, opportunities to play school sports and have equal entree into colleges and universities and professions once dominated by men. But it's time for us girls to regroup and get energized, because that first wave of feminist leaders seems to have achieved their goals as professionals but their successors lost steam. For example, in 1978, 100,000 women marched on Washington demanding equal rights. Currently called, "The Women's Equality Amendment," it still hasn't passed.

The Women's Movement also needs a course correction because it clearly failed when it came to protecting women as mothers. The current Web site of the National Organization of Women lists six top priority issues -- none of them directly involving mothers -- and of the twenty other important issues, only two of which, "Family Law" and "Mothers/Caregivers Rights," directly impact mothers.

In endless political debates, there's much talk about "bearing arms" and nothing about "bearing children." Lots of sententious palaver about the rights of the unborn, but nothing about what's due to the child that embryo will become. Like healthcare. In Washington our lawmakers have consistently and vociferously voted to protect some wildly unattractive (scary even) animal species they've never seen in person. How tough should it be to prompt them into protecting mothers when everyone in Congress has one?

I never was convinced, even back in the '70s, that the feminist leaders appropriately appreciated the gravitational pull of motherhood for most women. Because you really can't fool Mother Nature, the pressure to reproduce will always be a driving force, and motherhood is not a trivial role. Just look at the incredible lengths women these days go through to bear a child. Fertility specialists. In-vitro fertilization. Thousands of dollars spent to achieve what, ironically, most of their mothers tried to avoid.

Family is still the core value of most societies and mothers are its backbone. As a species, we are mammals who receive our first food from the bodies of the mothers who gave birth to us. And whose survival depends on mother and child being nourished and sheltered. A mother is the most powerful person in a child's life and as that child's foremost protector she needs defending. Lip service is given to motherhood as "the most important job a woman can have" and children as "the hope of the future," but the tax breaks go to the oil companies. As our feminist leaders marched forward, the problems of American mothers, particularly working mothers, have been largely ignored.

The last census revealed that over 1,300,000 babies were born that year to single mothers, and four out of five of them had to cope on less than $35,000 a year. When you also recognize that most two-parent families are dependent on dual incomes, it's obvious that our current laws do not begin to meet the needs of working families. In August '07, *National Geographic* reported that 170 countries offer paid maternity leave, and ninety-eight of them offer at least fourteen weeks off with pay. The United States is not one of them. In fact, we are one of only four countries with no paid family leave, putting us in the fashionable company of Papua New Guinea, Liberia and Swaziland.

There's more bad news. Achieving better equality in education and professions has not made women more contented. A recent Princeton study has found that there is now a growing happiness gap between men and women. In the early 1970s women reported being slightly happier than men. Today, in the wake of the Women's Movement, with two-thirds of American mothers working outside the home, the two have changed places. Since the 1960s men have gradually cut back on activities they find unpleasant, but over the same period, women have taken on paid-work but are still are spending almost as much time as they used to on homemaking.

The big reason that women reported being happier three decades ago is probably that they had lower expectations and more defined roles. This doesn't mean they were better off back then, but it shows how incomplete the gender revolution has been. American women have flooded into the workforce but American society hasn't fully come to grips with the repercussions. Because, unlike other industrialized countries, the United States still doesn't have universal preschool or the aforementioned guaranteed paid leave for parents. What has changed is that women who are mothers now have a much more responsibility than they once had, and can't possibly get it all done, so they end up feeling discouraged and exhausted. The Pushmi-Pullyu of working motherhood is overwhelming, particularly for the predominantly lower and middle-class women who are overworked and overlooked.

The other aspect of the Women's Movement, which hurt in the long run, was the presumed hostility to men. One of their famous mottos was, "A woman without a man is like a fish without a bicycle." It's cute but sets a dangerous tone. Men are not women's natural enemies. They are our fathers and brothers, our sons and lovers. Dr. Lionel Tiger wrote, "In the inexplicit and undeclared war between the sexes, women are on the way to winning, but the conditions of victory may not be agreeable. The armistice agreement may contain conditions no one wanted or expected. At the very least, the contestants don't have separate countries to which to return ... If liberation means the absence of unavoidable irrefutable obligations, women's liberation has backfired. It is men who have been liberated. They needn't be husbands or fathers to assure themselves of social status. They can be ex-husbands and part-time fathers."

Another keen observation from Dr. Tiger is, "housewife and mother have become uncomfortable and even embarrassing answers to the ubiquitous and quintessential twentieth century question, 'what do you do'?" It always makes me cringe when I 'Google' my name and the first page says, "Housewife turns feminist when husband leaves her." Because I never saw being a homemaker and being a feminist as mutually exclusive. I wanted to be a stay-at-home mother raising my five children because I felt it was the only job in the universe that I could do better than anyone else. If labels are important, I would not qualify as a feminist which is defined as someone who believes the sexes are equal. Because I don't. I have come to believe that women are not equal but superior, which I suppose makes me an uber-feminist.

Even before I began to get mail from stranded mothers and became aware of the depth of their problems, most of my personal heroes were mothers. Women in my life who unselfishly sacrificed without complaint for their children. One of my friends is a doctor who watched helplessly as her two young sons died of AIDS after receiving blood transfusions. She took her grief and turned it into resolve, founding an orphanage and hospital in sub-Sahara Africa devoted to AIDS victims. Less dramatic but no less heroic, is another old friend left widowed with five young children and very little else, who somehow managed to raise them into admirable adults and never even grumbled. Bertolt Brecht may have the copyright on the title, "Mother Courage" but we all know its true meaning.

Mothers are the backbone of our society and I don't understand why all of us who care about protecting mothers and strengthening families aren't lobbying our elected officials to make the changes necessary to bring our family-oriented laws in line with those in other developed countries. And not with piece-meal changes, but with a major overhaul. Otherwise we are doing what my Irish grandmother called, "pasting feathers together hoping for a duck."

# CHAPTER 18
## Evolution and Devolution

It has puzzled me that currently, with couples over fifty, sixty-five percent of divorces are originated by women. Although that same study I referred to earlier, (Luanne Brizendine's *The Female Brain*) provided some clarity asserting that in menopause, as estrogen levels fall, women may derive less pleasure from nurturing and more from independence. Which may help explain why older women, left alone by widowhood or divorce, seldom want to remarry.

The acclaimed Swedish writer Bodil Malmsten wrote, "the endless waiting for men that women of my generation have let themselves be subjected to ... what I might have achieved if I'd been spared the insane waiting for men. First for them to come along and then for them to leave."

One of my favorite maxims is that, "behind every successful man is an astonished mother-in-law." And I've come to appreciate that behind many a successful woman is a man who dumped her. I am a big fan of Madeline Albright, and in her autobiography she wrote about facing the uncomfortable idea that, if her husband had not left her for a younger woman, she would never have become Secretary of State. Every one of my AFGO group is better off, more productive and happier than she was before the divorce. But it took time. Most of the readers who shared their experiences with me still have raw wounds, but those who've healed pronounce themselves happier than ever before.

Which is not to say they don't mourn what they lost, and might rather have stayed in happy marriages and had those GE commercial kinds of golden-pond years waltzing around the kitchen with their men. Like most of them, I have happy memories. I had a wonderful marriage for more than thirty years -- a lovely home, great children, good friends and a husband who shared passion and joy.

I watch older couples squabbling in shops and restaurants, or worse yet, not saying a word to each other, and I feel relieved that I don't have to endure that. Then I watch others hugging or holding hands and I'm consumed with envy. Almost every day since I was handed those divorce papers, there is something that comes up where I have to bring myself up short and say, LET IT GO. Self-pity is such a satisfactory and warming emotion but it doesn't get you where you want to be. Like picking at a painful scab it does more harm than good.

When the ultimate destination is preordained, take the high road ... the low road is invariably more muddied anyway. Presiding as mayor I learned some helpful tricks. To present a calm countenance while being attacked by irate constituents at Board meetings, I learned to tuck my tongue behind my upper front teeth, which results in a serene smile with no hint of a smirk. It came in handy when my former in-laws spoke to me for the first time in ten years at my ex-husband's funeral. I was also incredibly grateful that insincerity doesn't have an odor.

We all want to be happy, but we can sabotage ourselves with self-inflicted rage and stress. Our constitution guarantees us the "pursuit of happiness"... it doesn't (and can't) promise individual happiness. I had to accept the truth that happiness for me was no longer an entitlement, but a choice I had to make every day to love life. It's said that cynicism is idealism betrayed, but mostly it's a downer. Arlene Dahl has a great motto, "love life and life will love you back." It works.

In his book, *Stumbling On Happiness*, Daniel Gilbert reports that research is clear that your mother was right -- money cannot buy happiness. Money is critical if you are living in poverty, but once your basic needs are met it won't increase your happiness much. It may even hurt if it keeps you so busy earning and spending, that it diverts time from your family and friends.

Money can help buy good health, and for men it can get you a better-looking wife, and if you get in trouble with the law, there's no denying that money is the most accepted proof of innocence. But there is evidence that happiness can come as much from giving as receiving, although happiness is partly inborn and no amount of money can buy you a naturally good disposition. It does, of course, offer you options, which is probably the reason Dostoyevsky claimed that money is "coined liberty." But basically money is only important when you don't have enough of it.

I was faced with an entirely new outlook on money and happiness when my husband scuttled our love boat. He swam to an exciting new place while I clung to the wreckage. But after a few terrible months I grew to embrace the idea that, for me, failure was not an option. I discovered just how little money I needed to exist in my newly simplified life.

Finances notwithstanding, if I had allowed myself to be destroyed by his abandonment, I would be letting my children down and, strangely enough, my long-dead parents. I felt a prideful responsibility to overcome the adversities facing me -- treat them like AFGOs -- and force myself to maximize the years I had left. And I may have overshot that runway. I didn't just change, I transformed into a determined, focused and unstoppable galivanter. My children's mantras went from, "you have to get out of the house," to, "don't you ever stay home?" I had been forced into making a life change I'd never envisioned, and have had more fun than I could have imagined.

Everyone knows that the rules and mores are shifting. But, as I mentioned before, basic human nature remains pretty much untouched as far back as the most primitive dictums. The first of Buddha's Four Noble Truths is "Life is suffering." This concept can offer consolation if you accept the premise that when you have a bad day, it's to be expected. And when you have a good day, it's a gift. My father never knew much about Buddha but he taught us, "blessed are those who expect little because they're so seldom disappointed."

Like my AFGO friends, I didn't just change, I evolved. There's a lot of that going around. It took a while -- millions of years actually -- but now the ultimate evolution of men seems to be happening. In 2005, the journal *Nature* published research revealing that women are more complex than scientists ever imagined, while men remain the simple creatures they appear. Genetically speaking, if you've met one man you've met them all. I profoundly hope they didn't pay a lot of money for that news.

But perhaps in this twenty-first century, men will finally come into their own by becoming more like women. Scientifically their

Y-chromosomes are shrinking to the extent that the English geneticist Steve Jones says males have devolved to become "the second sex." To a "vive la difference" girl like me that is not good news. But in all honesty, women are aiding this androgyny by becoming more like men as well, taking up contact sports and wearing baseball hats and getting tattooed. And, assuming some of their traditional weaknesses as they pick up some of ours.

Also the parameters of male and female are blurring. "Metrosexual" is a new designation for an urban heterosexual male who fusses with his appearance like a woman. He gets a manicure and has his hair styled and colored. His social priorities are more blithe than butch. He'd rather go to a fashion show than a prizefight. Further proof that this evolution/devolution thing is bringing the sexes closer together in bizarre ways.

It always seemed anatomically illogical that men rode astride a horse and women rode sidesaddle ... the trauma to male genitalia is bad enough on a bike but a horse! And why did men wear trousers and women wear skirts when it should be the other way around? Puzzling, but I figured that men, (except for the self-confident Scots) being so proud of their "packages" couldn't show them off under a dirndl and women having the more shapely legs had something going with skirts. They could flaunt their well-turned ankles. They had no desire to show off their genitals, it was enough to sport an alluring décolletage, since it seems most males have never been effectively weaned from the breast.

But for the first time in the history of women's fashion, in the last decade, women have begun to flaunt their genitals as much as you can show off what are basically internal facilities. They are wearing thongs, which looks like wedgies gone amuck to me. So revealing. So irritating. Jeans called "low rise" which means any lower and they needn't bother wearing anything at all. They get bikini waxes that are actually a form of torture, dormant since the Inquisition. And it defies logic that as part of being liberated from the traditional role of sex object, young women are wearing shoes with heels so spiked they have to totter about, constantly pitched forward in a kind of perpetual tripping mode. Talk about turned ankles.

The old clichés about roles in marriage are passé. Turned upside down and backwards. There once was the "henpecked" husband and the neglected wife. Wives were at home waiting for their children and husbands. Now husbands and children are waiting for them. Once men made money, parceling it out to women who spent it. Undoubtedly, mine was the last generation of married women to totally depend on men for their financial support.

Still I've often thought that luring young mothers into the workforce had some of the same elements as Tom Sawyer getting his chums to paint the fence by pretending it was fun. So I am not surprised that we now have the phenomenon of women achieving great success in the professional world, then giving it up to return to their homes and children. Female priorities are different than males, and those priorities are deeply ingrained and only marginally impacted by trends. Twenty-first century women still harbor deep-seated desires to give birth to babies and protect and nurture them.

Regardless of trends, mores have changed forever. When I was in college it was perfectly acceptable to iron a shirt for your boyfriend, but you'd slap his face if he asked you to go to bed with him. Today, it's ok for him to ask you to have sex but you'd slap his face if he suggested you iron his shirt. Seems to me that this is another more than fair tradeoff for most guys.

Right now we are in the midst of incredible flux, a sexual identity shift which is especially disconcerting, because life itself, before all these social changes, was tough enough. I have a friend whose Italian uncle met every one of his complaints ... about kindergarten, high school, college, law school, with, "don't worry Aldo. It'll get worse." And he was a prophet. Most of us plow on realizing that pain is inevitable but hoping for the best ... searching out opportunities for growth and pleasure. What gets in the way is anger and resentment so they have to be shoved aside. Why would you want to slog through life hauling bags of garbage behind you?

There are unfortunate individuals in our society who are always angry. They idle at furious. So their lives are unproductive, friendless and miserable. After my divorce, when I was elected mayor of Nyack, I became a target for several of them. As the first woman mayor I had some sexist enemies who, on the eve of my re-election posted cruel notices around the Village saying, "DUMP TERRY HEKKER... PAID FOR BY THE PEOPLE WHO THINK JACK HEKKER WAS

RIGHT." That brutally wounded me and my children, and it was harrowing until I realized I was allowing people I could never respect to rent space in my head. Given what the divorce had already done to my self-esteem, I would not have survived if I allowed their unflagging criticism and hatred ruin my life. And I refused to become obsessed with exacting murderous revenge, although I occasionally hoped they would eat a bad clam.

Oscar Wilde said, "Always pass on good advice. It is the only thing to do with it. It is never any use to oneself." And so I leave you with some things I learned the hard way in seven decades. The best metaphor I know for life is Woody Allen's story, which begins his great movie *Annie Hall*. Two old Jewish ladies are having lunch at a Catskill resort and one says, "the food here is awful." The other one replies, "yes, and such small portions."

Life is often terrible and always too short. We are each dealt a hand, often most unfairly, and must play the hand we're dealt. I had to concentrate on putting aside thoughts of what I'd lost and focusing with gratitude on what I had left. We all face disappointment and fractured illusions and crushed dreams. And, we are forced to deal with situations that can never be happily resolved.

There are people in our lives who betray and wound us and make it tough to hold our heads up. I have found it's best to take the high road and keep smiling. And in this imperfect world we can try to forgive, but a just God will allow us some antipathy. So in the worst of times, I was able to take great comfort from an Irish prayer passed on to me by my angelic ninety-two year old Aunt Nora:

MAY THOSE WHO LOVE US, LOVE US
AND THOSE THAT DON'T LOVE US,
MAY GOD TURN THEIR HEARTS
AND IF HE DOES NOT TURN THEIR HEARTS
MAY HE TURN THEIR ANKLES
SO WE WILL KNOW THEM BY THEIR LIMPING.

# FINALE

CONGRATULATIONS!

Thank you for finishing my book. Eleven publishers said you wouldn't ... that nobody would. So you deserve a reward and here it is. A real treasure, my grandmother O'Donohue's recipe for Irish Soda Bread. It is the "poor Irish" version in that it doesn't call for yeast or eggs. It takes minutes to make and is delicious just out of the oven and the next day and the next day, if there's still some left, as toast.

Grandmother O'Donohue's Irish Soda Bread

In a large bowl combine:

6 cups of unsifted white flour
1 quart of buttermilk
1 15 oz. box of raisins
2 flat teaspoons of baking soda
2 heaping teaspoons of baking powder
2 tablespoons of caraway seeds
1 tablespoon of sugar
1 tablespoon of salt

Mix thoroughly with a wooden spoon. Heap into two rounded mounds* onto a greased cookie sheet. Bake at 350 for 1 hour. You can drizzle melted butter on top as it bakes but that's not required if you're too busy.

*Resist any urge to smooth them out, as you want them spiky.

Note:
I was tempted to also give the recipe for the 'Pot Roast That Killed Grandpa', but I'm not sure the statute of limitations has run out.

THE END

# ACKNOWLEDGEMENTS

I owe so much to so many that I can't possibly list them all. But I must recognize my amazing immediate family; Jack, Julie, Peter, Mary Ellen, Michael, Reba, Paul, Annie and Tommy, who provide the wind beneath my tattered wings. And have given me twelve priceless gifts. Abundant gratitude to my extraordinary Martin and O'Donohue relatives who I love beyond words (and who provided most of the material), and to my patient friends who've suffered through this process with me.

Also, I must identify the three people without whose help I could not have produced this book. First, Donald Stannard, whose friendship, support and willingness to accompany me to bizarre engagements, was beyond gracious. Second, Clea Carchia, who handles my Web site, designed the book covers and took a picture of twenty-two people and a dog all with their eyes opened. And third, but most significant of all, to Mary Lukens, my editor, agent and sounding board for her incredible professionalism and unstinting encouragement.

# BIOGRAPHY

In 1976, Terry Martin Hekker was a fortyish housewife with five children when she wrote an Op-Ed column for *The New York Times* defending her choice to be a stay-at-home mother. But her world crashed in 1996 when, after a forty-year marriage, her husband divorced her. After an initial period of despair and humiliation, she decided to take life head-on, becoming the first women elected mayor of her small Hudson Valley village of Nyack.

Then on New Year's Day 2006, *The New York Times* ran a piece by Terry about her divorce and recovery in their Modern Love column which echoed around the world. Terry still lives in Nyack, is active in her community and kept busy by a large and boisterous family. She can be contacted at terry.hekker@verizon.net.